NAPOLEON HILL'S
GOLDEN
CLASSICS

Think and Grow Rich

———◆———

The Law of Success

———◆———

The Master Key to Riches

ABRIDGED AND INTRODUCED BY
MITCH

T0165591

▼
MEDIA

Published by Gildan Media LLC
aka G&D Media.
www.GandDmedia.com

Think and Grow Rich was originally published in 1937
The Law of Success was originally published in 1928
The Master Key to Riches was originally published in 1945
G&D Media Condensed Classics editions published 2018
Abridgement and Introduction copyright © 2018 by Mitch
Horowitz

FIRST EDITION: 2018

Cover design by David Rheinhardt of Pyrographx

Interior design by Meghan Day Healey of Story Horse, LLC.

ISBN: 978-1-7225-0089-4

Contents

Introduction

The Power of Brevity
By Mitch Horowitz

If you're anything like me, you're turned off by labels like "condensed" or "abridged" on a book. You want the full experience. So, when I accepted the challenge of introducing and abridging a series of Napoleon Hill's classics of self development, I asked myself: Can I approach this task with integrity? And can I preserve the completeness of Hill's program, while reducing it to its essentials?

In experiencing this volume—which includes *Think and Grow Rich*, *The Law of Success*, and *The Master Key to Riches*—I believe you'll share my confidence that the answer is yes.

As a seeker, chronicler, and historian of the metaphysical, I personally treasure the works of Napoleon Hill. His ideas have immeasurably improved my life. Hence, I threw myself into this task with considerable care and passion. I personally believe that these are the finest abridgements of Hill that can be found. (I write this with apologies to one my heroes, narrator and motivational writer Earl Nightingale, who creditably abridged *Think and Grow Rich* in 1960. Due to the manners and morals of the era, Earl downplayed Hill's writing on sex energy, which is fully and clearly explored here.) I hope, too, that my individual introductions to each of these separate volumes deepen their impact.

But the question lingers: Why abridge these highly readable works at all? Is this volume just a crass act of commercialism, or a needless truncating of practical wisdom? No. It is something much, much more than that.

There are two essentials to succeeding with Hill's program. First, you must use his techniques fully and completely, omitting nothing. (You will find no key step absent here.) Second, and vital to our purposes, you must *review* the master's material again and again, so that it becomes second nature. It must change how you think. That is where these abridgments possess special value. Each serves as a primer or refresher of Hill's ideas, and each is easily digestible within a *single sitting*. What's more, these compact editions serve as wonderful *introductions* to Hill's work, so that if you've heard of *Think and Grow*, or other of his books, and have wanted to dip into them but haven't found the time, here is your opportunity. Or, finally, if you're trying to introduce a friend, colleague or loved one to the work of

Hill and are meeting with resistance or procrastination, these digest-sized editions are a perfect entry point.

I mentioned two keys to using Hill's work: *thoroughness* and *review*. But, actually, there is another, hidden key—and it holds the secret, if there is one, to benefiting from Hill's program, and from any legitimate program of self-development. And that is: *absolute passion*. I believe with all my heart and intellect—as well as from the perspective of personal experience— that if you approach this volume with hunger and steely determination for self-improvement, you will not come away unchanged.

These short works are the keys to a better, more productive, more purposeful, and more remunerative existence. But *passion* is the vital turnkey. If you possess it, let's begin together to newly explore life and its possibilities.

THINK
AND
GROW RICH

THINK AND GROW RICH

by Napoleon Hill

The Original 1937 Classic
Abridged and Introduced
by Mitch Horowitz

THE CONDENSED CLASSICS LIBRARY™

Contents

The Power of a Single Book

The book you are about to experience has probably touched more lives than any other work of modern self-help. Try a small personal experiment: Carry a copy of *Think and Grow Rich* with you through an airport, grocery store, shopping mall, or any public place—and see if more than one person doesn't stop you and say something like, "Now, *that's* a great book . . ."

I have met artists, business people, doctors, teachers, athletes—people from different professions and possessed of seemingly different outer goals—who have attested that *Think and Grow Rich* made a concrete difference in their lives.

This is because, whatever our individual aims and desires, all motivated people share one common trait: the drive for personal excellence. This book, better than any other I know, breaks down the steps and elements to accomplishing any worthy goal.

When journalist Napoleon Hill published *Think and Grow Rich* in 1937 he had already dedicated more than twenty years of study to discovering and documenting the common traits displayed by high achievers across varying fields. Hill observed and interviewed more than five hundred exceptional people, ranging from statesmen and generals, to inventors and industrialists.

He condensed their shared traits into thirteen principles of accomplishment—and this forms the core of *Think and Grow Rich*.

This book has sold many millions of copies around the world since its first appearance—but that is not the true measure of its success. Lots of books gain popularity for a time, but go unread and sometimes unheard of within a decade or so of their publication. But *Think and Grow Rich* has, if anything, grown in influence since Hill's death in 1970. Its ideas are at the foundation of most of today's philosophies of business motivation and personal achievement.

But there is still more to Hill's book than that—and this brings us back to the little experiment proposed at the start of this preface. *Think and Grow Rich* evokes rare and deeply felt affection among many of its readers. All over America, and in other parts of the world, it is possible to run into friendly strangers who will beckon you aside for a moment to share a brief personal connection, telling you how *Think and Grow Rich* has helped them in life.

In a sense, you are about to join an informal fraternity of strivers, from a wide range of backgrounds, who have benefited from the principles in this book. When you meet them—and you will—many will welcome you with a nod and a smile, as if to say: *We've been waiting for you*.

—Mitch Horowitz

CHAPTER ONE

Desire
The First Step to Riches

In the early twentieth century a great American salesman and businessman named Edwin C. Barnes discovered how true it is that men really do *think and grow rich*.

Barnes's discovery did not come in one sitting. It came little by little, beginning with an ALL-CONSUMING DESIRE to become a business associate of inventor Thomas Edison. One of the chief characteristics of Barnes's desire was that it was *definite*. Barnes wanted to work *with* Edison—not just *for* him.

Straight off a freight train, Barnes presented himself in 1905 at Edison's New Jersey laboratory. He announced that he had come to go into business with the inventor. In speaking of their meeting years later, Edison said: "He stood there before me, looking like an ordinary tramp, but there was something in the expression of his face which conveyed the impression that he was determined to get what he had come after."

Barnes did *not* get his partnership with Edison on his first interview. But he *did* get a chance to work in the Edison offices, at a very nominal wage, doing a job that was unimportant to Edison—but *most important* to Barnes, because it gave him an opportunity to display his abilities to his future "partner."

Months passed. Nothing happened outwardly to bring Barnes any closer to his goal. But something important *was* happening in Barnes's mind. He was constantly intensifying his CHIEF DESIRE and his PLANS to become Edison's business associate.

Barnes was DETERMINED TO REMAIN READY UNTIL HE GOT THE OPPORTUNITY HE CAME FOR.

When the "big chance" arrived, it was in a different form, and from a different direction, than Barnes had expected. *That is one of the tricks of opportunity.* It has a sly habit of slipping in by the back door, and it often comes disguised as misfortune or temporary defeat. Perhaps this is why so many fail to wait for—or recognize—opportunity when it arrives.

Edison had just perfected a new device, known then as the Edison Dictating Machine. His salesmen were not enthusiastic. But Barnes saw his opportunity hidden in a strange-looking contraption that interested no one. Barnes seized the chance to sell the dictating machine, and did it so successfully that Edison gave him a contract to distribute and market it all over the world.

When Edwin C. Barnes climbed down from that freight train in Orange, New Jersey, he possessed one CONSUMING OBSESSION: to become the business associate of the great inventor. Barnes's desire was not a *hope!* It was not a *wish!* It was a keen, pulsating DESIRE, which transcended everything else. It was DEFINITE.

Wishing will not bring riches or other forms of success. But *desiring* riches with a state of mind that becomes an obsession, then planning definite ways and means to acquire riches, and backing those plans with persistence *that does not recognize failure*, will bring success.

The method by which DESIRE can be transmuted into its financial equivalent, consists of six definite, practical steps.

FIRST

Fix in your mind the *exact* amount of money you desire. It is not sufficient merely to say, "I want plenty of money." Be definite as to the amount.

SECOND

Determine exactly what you intend to give in return for the money you desire.

THIRD

Establish a definite date when you intend to *possess* the money you desire.

FOURTH

Create *a definite plan* for carrying out your desire, and begin *at once*, whether or not you are ready, to put this plan into *action*.

FIFTH

Write out a clear, concise statement of the amount of money you intend to acquire, name the time limit for its acquisition, state what you intend to give in return for the money, and describe clearly the plan through which you intend to accumulate it.

SIXTH

Read your written statement aloud, twice daily, once just before retiring at night and once after arising in the morning. AS YOU READ—SEE AND FEEL AND BELIEVE YOURSELF ALREADY IN POSSESSION OF THE MONEY.

It is especially important that you observe and follow number six. You may complain that it is impossible for you to "see yourself in possession of money" before you actually have it. Here is where a BURNING DESIRE will come to your aid. If you truly DESIRE money or another goal so keenly that your desire is an obsession, you will have no difficulty in convincing yourself that you will acquire it. The object is to want it so much and become so determined that you CONVINCE yourself you will have it. In future chapters you will learn why this is so important.

CHAPTER TWO

Faith
The Second Step to Riches

FAITH is the head chemist of the mind. When FAITH is blended with the vibration of thought, the subconscious mind instantly picks up the vibration, translates it into its spiritual equivalent, and transmits it to Infinite Intelligence, as in the case of prayer.

ALL THOUGHTS THAT HAVE BEEN EMOTIONALIZED (given feeling) AND MIXED WITH FAITH begin immediately to translate themselves into their physical equivalent.

If you have difficulty getting a grasp of just what faith is, think of it as a special form of *persistence*—one that we feel when we *know* that we have right at our backs and that helps us persevere through setbacks and temporary failure.

To develop this quality in yourself, use this five-step formula. Promise yourself to read, repeat, and abide by these steps—and write down your promise.

FIRST
I know that I have the ability to achieve the object of my DEFINITE PURPOSE in life, therefore, I *demand* of myself persistent, continuous action toward its attainment, and I here and now promise to render such action.

SECOND
I realize the dominating thoughts of my mind will eventually reproduce themselves in outward physical action, and gradually transform themselves into physical reality. Therefore, I will concentrate my thoughts for thirty minutes daily upon the task of thinking of the person I intend to become, thereby creating in my mind a clear mental picture of that person.

THIRD
I know that through the principle of auto suggestion any desire that I persistently hold in my mind will eventually seek expression through some practical means of attaining the object back of it. Therefore, I will devote ten minutes daily to demanding of myself the development of *self-confidence*.

FOURTH

I have clearly written down a description of my DEFI-NITE CHIEF AIM in life, and I will never stop trying until I have developed sufficient self-confidence for its attainment.

FIFTH

I fully realize that no wealth or position can long endure unless built upon truth and justice. Therefore, I will engage in no transaction which does not benefit all whom it affects. I will succeed by attracting to myself the forces I wish to use, and the cooperation of other people. I will induce others to serve me, because of my willingness to serve others. I will eliminate hatred, envy, jealousy, self-ishness, and cynicism, by developing love for all human-ity, because I know that a negative attitude toward others can never bring me success. I will cause others to believe in me because I will believe in them, and in myself.

I will sign my name to this formula, commit it to mem-ory, and repeat it aloud once a day, with full FAITH that it will gradually influence my THOUGHTS and ACTIONS, so that I will become a self-reliant and suc-cessful person.

CHAPTER THREE

Auto Suggestion
The Third Step to Riches

AUTO SUGGESTION is a term that applies to all suggestions and self-administered stimuli that reach one's mind through the five senses. Stated another way: *auto suggestion is self suggestion*.

It is the agency of communication between the conscious and subconscious minds. But your subconscious mind recognizes and acts ONLY upon thoughts that have been well mixed with *emotion or feeling*. This is a fact of such importance as to warrant repetition.

When you begin to use—and keep using—the three-step program for auto suggestion in this chapter, be on the alert for hunches from your subconscious mind—and when they appear, put them into ACTION IMMEDIATELY.

FIRST

Go into some quiet spot (preferably in bed at night) where you will not be disturbed or interrupted, close your eyes, and repeat aloud (so you may hear your own words) the written statement of the amount of money you intend to accumulate, the time limit for its accumulation, and a description of the service or merchandise you intend to give in return for the money. As you carry out these instructions SEE YOURSELF ALREADY IN POSSESSION OF THE MONEY.

For example: Suppose that you intend to accumulate $50,000 by the first of January, five years hence, and that you intend to give personal services in return for the money in the capacity of a salesman. Your written statement of your purpose should be similar to the following:

"By the first day of January, I will have in my possession $50,000, which will come to me in various amounts from time to time during the interim.

"In return for this money I will give the most efficient service of which I am capable, rendering the fullest possible quantity and the best possible quality of service in the capacity of salesman of …(and describe the service or merchandise you intend to sell).

"I believe that I will have this money in my possession. My faith is so strong that I can now see this money before my eyes. I can touch it with my hands. It is now awaiting transfer to me at the time and in the proportion that I deliver the service I intend to render for it. I am awaiting a plan by which to accumulate this money, and I will follow that plan when it is received."

SECOND

Repeat this program night and morning until you can see (in your imagination) the money you intend to accumulate.

THIRD

Place a written copy of your statement where you can see it night and morning, and read it just before retiring and upon arising, until it has been memorized.

Chapter Four

Specialized Knowledge
The Fourth Step to Riches

Geneal knowledge, no matter how great in quantity or variety, is of little use in accumulating money. Knowledge is only *potential* power. It becomes power only when, and if, it is organized into *definite plans of action,* and directed toward a *definite end.*

In connection with your aim, you must decide what sort of specialized knowledge you require, and the purpose for which it is needed. To a large extent, your major purpose in life, and the goal toward which you are working, will help determine what knowledge you need. With this question settled, your next move requires that you have ACCURATE INFORMATION concerning DEPENDABLE SOURCES OF KNOWLEDGE.

Look toward many high-quality sources for the knowledge you seek: people, courses, partnerships, books—look everywhere. Some of this knowledge will be free—never undervalue what is free—and some will require purchasing. Decide what knowledge you seek—and pursue it completely. The author spent more than twenty years interviewing people and studying success methods before writing this book.

Without specialized knowledge, your ideas remain mere wishes. Once you have acquired the knowledge you need, you can use your critical faculty of *imagination* to combine your IDEAS with this SPECIALIZED KNOWLEDGE, and make ORGANIZED PLANS to carry out your aims.

This is the formula for capability: *Using imagination to combine specialized knowledge with ideas and to form organized plans.*

The connecting ingredient is imagination, which we will now learn to cultivate.

CHAPTER FIVE

Imagination
The Fifth Step to Riches

The imagination is the workshop wherein are fashioned all plans created by man. The impulse, the DESIRE, is literally given shape, form, and ACTION through the aid of the imaginative faculty of the mind.

Through the medium of creative imagination, the finite mind of man has direct communication with Infinite Intelligence. Imagination is the faculty through which "hunches" and "inspirations" are reached. It is by this faculty that all basic or new ideas are handed over to man. It is through this faculty that thought vibrations from the minds of others are received. It is through this faculty that one individual may "tune in" or communicate with the subconscious minds of others.

The creative imagination works only when the conscious mind is stimulated through the emotion of a STRONG DESIRE. This is highly significant.

What's more, the creative faculty may have become weak through inaction. Your imagination becomes more alert and more receptive in proportion to its development through *use*.

After you have completed this book, return to this section and begin at once to put your imagination to work on the building of a plan, or plans, for the transmutation of *desire* into money, or your core aim. Reduce your plan to writing. The moment you complete this, you will have *definitely* given concrete form to the intangible *desire*.

This step is extremely important. When you reduce the statement of your desire, and a plan for its realization, into writing, you have actually *taken the first* of a series of steps that will enable you to covert your *thought* into its physical counterpart.

Chapter Six

Organized Planning
The Sixth Step to Riches

It is vital that you form a DEFINITE, practical plan, or plans, to carry out your aims. You will now learn how to build plans that are *practical*, as follows:

FIRST
Ally yourself with a group of as many people as you may need for the creation and carrying out of your plan or plans for the accumulation of money—making use of the "Master Mind" principle described in a later chapter. (Compliance with this instruction is essential. Do not neglect it.)

SECOND
Before forming your "Master Mind" alliance, decide what advantages and benefits you may offer the indi-

vidual members of your group in return for their co-operation. No one will work indefinitely without some form of compensation. No intelligent person will either request or expect another to work without adequate compensation, although this may not always be in the form of money.

THIRD

Arrange to meet with the members of your "Master Mind" group at least twice a week, and more often if possible, until you have jointly perfected the necessary plan or plans for the accumulation of money.

FOURTH

Maintain *perfect harmony* between yourself and every member of your "Master Mind" group. If you fail to carry out this instruction to the letter, you may expect to meet with failure. The "Master Mind" principle *cannot* obtain where *perfect harmony* does not prevail.

Keep in mind these facts:

1. You are engaged in an undertaking of major importance to you. To be sure of success, you must have plans that are faultless.

2. You must have the advantage of the experience, education, native ability, and imagination of other

minds. This is in harmony with the methods followed by every person who has accumulated a great fortune.

Now, if the first plan you devise does not work successfully, replace it with a new plan. If this new plan fails to work, replace it, in turn, with still another, and so on, until you find a plan that *does work*. Right here is the point where the majority of men meet with failure, because of their lack of *persistence* in creating new plans to take the place of those that fail.

Remember this when your plans fail: *Temporary defeat is not permanent failure.*

No follower of this philosophy can reasonably expect to accumulate a fortune without experiencing "temporary defeat." When defeat comes, accept it as a signal that your plans are not sound, rebuild those plans, and set sail once more toward your goal.

Finally, as you are devising your plans keep in mind these Major Attributes of Leadership—traits possessed by the greatest achievers:

1. Unwavering Courage
2. Self-Control
3. A Keen Sense of Justice
4. Definiteness of Decision

5. Definiteness of Plans
6. The Habit of Doing More Than Paid For
7. A Pleasing Personality
8. Sympathy and Understanding
9. Mastery of Detail
10. Willingness to Assume Full Responsibility
11. Cooperation With Others

CHAPTER SEVEN

Decision
The Seventh Step to Riches

Analysis of several hundred people who had accumulated fortunes disclosed that *every one of them* had the habit of *reaching decisions promptly*, and of changing these decisions slowly, if and when they were changed. People who fail to accumulate money, *without exception*, have the habit of reaching decisions, if at all, very *slowly*, and of *changing these decisions quickly and often*.

What's more, the majority of people who fail to accumulate money sufficient for their needs tend to be easily influenced by the "opinions" of others. "Opinions" are the cheapest commodities on earth. Everyone has a flock of opinions ready to be wished upon anyone who will accept them. If you are influenced by "opinions" when you reach *decisions*, you will not succeed in any undertaking, much less in that of transmuting *your own desire* into money.

If you are influenced by the opinions of others, you will have no DESIRE of your own.

Keep your own counsel when you begin to put into practice the principles described here by *reaching your own decisions* and following them. Take no one into your confidence *except* the members of your "Master Mind" group, and be very sure in your selection of this group that you choose ONLY those who will be in COMPLETE SYMPATHY AND HARMONY WITH YOUR PURPOSE.

Close friends and relatives, while not meaning to, often handicap one through "opinions" and sometimes through ridicule, which is meant to be humorous. Thousands of men and women carry inferiority complexes with them throughout life, because some well-meaning but ignorant person destroyed their confidence through "opinions" or ridicule.

You have a mind of your own. USE IT and reach your own decisions. If you need facts or information from others to enable you to reach decisions, as you probably will in many instances, acquire these facts or secure the information you need quietly, without disclosing your purpose.

Those who reach DECISIONS promptly and definitely know what they want and generally get it. Leaders in every walk of life DECIDE quickly and firmly. That is the major reason why they are leaders. The world has a habit of making room for the man whose words and actions show that he knows where he is going.

Chapter Eight

Persistence
The Eighth Step to Riches

P ERSITENCE is an essential factor in transmuting DESIRE into its monetary equivalent. The basis of persistence is the POWER OF WILL.

Will power and desire, when properly combined, make an irresistible pair. Men who accumulate great fortunes are generally known as cold-blooded and sometimes ruthless. Often they are misunderstood. What they have is will power, which they mix with persistence, and place at the back of their desires to *ensure* the attainment of their objectives.

Lack of persistence is one of the major causes of failure. Experience with thousands of people has proved that lack of persistence is a weakness common to the majority of men. It is a weakness that may be overcome by effort. The ease with which lack of persistence may be conquered depends *entirely* upon the INTENSITY OF ONE'S DESIRE.

In short, THERE IS NO SUBSTITUTE FOR PERSISTENCE! It cannot be supplanted by any other quality! Remember this and it will hearten you in the beginning when the going may seem difficult and slow.

Those who have cultivated the HABIT of persistence seem to enjoy insurance against failure. No matter how many times they are defeated, they finally arrive toward the top of the ladder. Sometimes it appears that there is a hidden Guide whose duty is to test men through all sorts of discouraging experiences. Those who pick themselves up after defeat and keep on trying arrive at their destination. The hidden Guide lets no one enjoy great achievement without passing the PERSISTENCE TEST.

What we DO NOT SEE, what most of us never suspect of existing, is the silent but irresistible POWER that comes to the rescue of those who fight on in the face of discouragement. If we speak of this power at all, we call it PERSISTENCE.

There are four simple steps that lead to the habit of PERSISTENCE.

1. A definite purpose backed by burning desire for its fulfillment.

2. A definite plan, expressed in continuous action.
3. A mind closed tightly against all negative and discouraging influences, including negative suggestions of relatives, friends, and acquaintances.
4. A friendly alliance with one or more persons who will encourage you to follow through with both plan and purpose.

Chapter Nine

The Master Mind
The Ninth Step to Riches

The "Master Mind" may be defined as: "Coordination of knowledge and effort, in a spirit of harmony, between two or more people for the attainment of a definite purpose."

No individual may hold great power without availing himself of the "Master Mind." A previous chapter supplied instructions for the creation of PLANS for the purpose of translating DESIRE into its monetary equivalent. If you carry out these instructions with PERSISTENCE and intelligence, and use discrimination in selecting your "Master Mind" group, your objective will have been halfway reached, even before you begin to recognize it.

The Master Mind brings an obvious economic advantage, by allowing you to surround yourself with the advice, counsel, and personal cooperation of a group of people who are willing to lend you wholehearted aid in a spirit of PERFECT HARMONY. But there is also a more abstract phase; it may be called the PSYCHIC PHASE.

The psychic phase of the Master Mind is more difficult to comprehend because it has reference to the spiritual forces with which the human race, as a whole, is not well acquainted. You may catch a significant suggestion from this statement: "No two minds ever come together without, thereby, creating a third invisible, intangible force which may be likened to a third mind."

The human mind is a form of energy, a part of it being spiritual in nature. When the minds of two people are coordinated in a SPIRIT OF HARMONY the spiritual units of energy of each mind form an affinity, which constitutes the "psychic" phase of the Master Mind.

Analyze the record of any man who has accumulated a great fortune, and many of those who have accumulated modest fortunes, and you will find that they have either consciously or unconsciously employed the "Master Mind."

Great power can be accumulated through no other principle!

Chapter Ten

Sex Transmutation
The Tenth Step to Riches

The meaning of the word "transmute" is, in simple language, "the changing or transferring of one element, or form of energy, into another." The emotion of sex brings into being a unique and powerful state of mind that can be used for extraordinary intellectual and material creative purposes.

This is accomplished through *sex transmutation*, which means the switching of the mind from thoughts of physical expression to thoughts of some other nature.

Sex is the most powerful of human desires. When driven by this desire, men develop keenness of imagination, courage, will power, persistence, and creative ability unknown to them at other times. So strong and impelling is the desire for sexual contact that men freely run the risk of life and reputation to indulge it.

When harnessed and redirected along other lines, this motivating force maintains all of its attributes of keenness of imagination, courage, etc., which may be used as powerful creative forces in literature, art, or in any other profession or calling, including, of course, the accumulation of riches.

The transmutation of sex energy calls for the exercise of will power, to be sure, but the reward is worth the effort. The desire for sexual expression is inborn and natural. The desire cannot, and should not, be submerged or eliminated. But it should be given an outlet through forms of expression that enrich the body, mind, and spirit. If not given this form of outlet, through transmutation, it will seek outlets through purely physical channels.

The emotion of sex is an "irresistible force." When driven by this emotion, men become gifted with a super power for action. Understand this truth, and you will catch the significance of the statement that sex transmutation will lift one into the status of a genius. The emotion of sex contains the secret of creative ability.

When harnessed and transmuted, this driving force is capable of lifting men to that higher sphere of thought which enables them to master the sources of worry and petty annoyance that beset their pathway on the lower plane.

The major reason why the majority of men who succeed do not begin to do so until after the ages of forty to fifty (or beyond), is their tendency to DISS-APTE their energies through over indulgence in physical expression of the emotion of sex. The majority of men *never* learn that the urge of sex has other possibilities, which far transcend in importance that of mere physical expression.

But remember, sexual energy must be *transmuted* from desire for physical contact into some *other* form of desire and action, in order to lift one to the status of a genius.

CHAPTER ELEVEN

The Subconscious Mind
The Eleventh Step to Riches

The subconscious mind is the connecting link between the finite mind of man and Infinite Intelligence. It is the intermediary through which one may draw upon the forces of Infinite Intelligence at will. It alone contains the secret process by which mental impulses are modified and changed into their spiritual equivalent. It alone is the medium through which prayer may be transmitted to the source capable of answering prayer.

I never approach the discussion of the subconscious mind without a feeling of littleness and inferiority due, perhaps, to the fact that man's entire stock of knowledge on the subject is so pitifully limited. The very fact that the subconscious mind is the medium of communication between the thinking mind of man and Infinite

Intelligence is, of itself, a thought that almost paralyzes one's reason.

After you have accepted as a reality the existence of your subconscious mind, and understand its possibilities for transmuting your DESIRES into their physical or monetary equivalent, you will understand why you have been repeatedly urged to MAKE YOUR DESIRES CLEAR, AND TO REDUCE THEM TO WRITING. You will also understand the necessity of PERSISTENCE in carrying out instructions.

The thirteen principles in this book are the stimuli with which—through practice and persistence—you acquire the ability to reach and influence your subconscious mind.

Chapter Twelve

The Brain
The Twelfth Step to Riches

More than twenty years before writing this book, the author, working with the late Dr. Alexander Graham Bell and Dr. Elmer R. Gates, observed that every human brain is both a broadcasting and receiving station for the vibration of thought.

The Creative Imagination is the "receiving set" of the brain, which receives thoughts released by the brains of others. It is the agency of communication between one's conscious, or reasoning, mind, and the outer sources from which one may receive thought stimuli.

When stimulated, or "stepped up," to a high rate of vibration, the mind becomes more receptive to the vibration of thought from outside sources. This "stepping up" occurs through the positive emotions or the negative emotions. Through the emotions the vibrations of thought may be increased. This is why it is crucial that your goal have strong emotions at the back of it.

Vibrations of an exceedingly high rate are the only vibrations picked up and carried from one brain to another. Thought is energy travelling at an exceedingly high rate of vibration. Thought that has been modified or "stepped up" by any of the major emotions vibrates at a much higher rate than ordinary thought, and it is this type of thought that passes from one mind to another, through the broadcasting machinery of the human brain.

Thus, you will see that the broadcasting principle is the factor through which you mix feeling or emotion with your thoughts and pass them on to your subconscious mind, or to the minds of others.

Chapter Thirteen

The Sixth Sense
The Thirteenth Step to Riches

The thirteenth and final principle is known as the "sixth sense," through which Infinite Intelligence may and will communicate voluntarily, without any effort or demands by the individual.

After you have mastered the principles in this book, you will be prepared to accept as true a statement that may otherwise seem incredible, namely: Through the aid of the sixth sense you will be warned of impending dangers in time to avoid them, and notified of opportunities in time to embrace them.

With the development of the sixth sense, there comes to your aid, and to do your bidding, a kind of "guardian angel" who will open to you at all times the door to the Temple of Wisdom.

Whether this is a statement of truth, you will never know except by following the instructions described in this book, or some similar method.

The author is not a believer in, nor an advocate of, "miracles," for the reason that he has enough knowledge of Nature to understand that Nature *never deviates from her established laws.* Some of her laws are so incomprehensible that they produce what appear to be "miracles."

The sixth sense comes as near to being a miracle as anything I have ever experienced.

A Word About Fear

As you begin any new undertaking you are likely at one point or another to find yourself gripped by the emotion of fear.

Fear should never be bargained with or capitulated to. It takes the charm from one's personality, destroys the possibility of accurate thinking, diverts concentration of effort, masters persistence, turns the will power into nothingness, destroys ambition, beclouds the memory, and invites failure in every conceivable form. It kills love, assassinates the finer emotions of the heart, discourages friendship, and leads to sleeplessness, misery, and unhappiness.

So pernicious and destructive is the emotion of fear that it is, almost literally, worse than anything that can befall you.

If you suffer from a fear of poverty, reach a decision to get along with whatever wealth you can accumulate WITHOUT WORRY. If you fear the loss of love, reach a decision to get along without love, if that is necessary. If you experience a general sense of worry, reach a blanket decision that *nothing* life has to offer is *worth* the price of worry.

And remember: The greatest of all remedies for fear is a BURNING DESIRE FOR ACHIEVEMENT, backed by useful service to others.

ABOUT THE AUTHORS

NAPOLEON HILL was born in 1883 in Wise County, Virginia. He was employed as a secretary, a reporter for a local newspaper, the manager of a coalmine and a lumberyard, and attended law school, before he began working as a journalist for *Bob Taylor's Magazine,* an inspirational and general-interest journal. In 1908 the job led to his interviewing steel magnate Andrew Carnegie. The encounter changed the course of Hill's life. Carnegie believed success could be distilled into principles that anyone could follow, and urged Hill to interview the greatest industrialists, financiers, and inventors of the era to discover these principles. Hill accepted the challenge, which lasted more than twenty years and formed the building block for *Think and Grow Rich.* Hill dedicated the rest of his life to documenting and refining the principles of success. After a long career as an author, magazine publisher, lecturer, and consultant to business leaders, the motivational pioneer died in 1970 in South Carolina.

MITCH HOROWITZ, who abridged and introduced this volume, is the PEN Award-winning author of books including *Occult America* and *The Miracle Club: How Thoughts Become Reality*. *The Washington Post* says Mitch "treats esoteric ideas and movements with an even-handed intellectual studiousness that is too often lost in today's raised-voice discussions." Follow him @MitchHorowitz.

THE LAW
OF SUCCESS

THE LAW
OF SUCCESS

by Napoleon Hill

The Original Classic

from the author of
Think and Grow Rich

Abridged and Introduced
by Mitch Horowitz

THE CONDENSED CLASSICS LIBRARY™

Contents

The Science of Success

Y ou are about to experience Napoleon Hill's first comprehensive exploration of the principles of success. Hill began this project when, as a young journalist, he interviewed industrialist Andrew Carnegie in 1908. Carnegie urged the writer to make an intensive study of leaders across diverse fields to determine whether high achievers share a set of common traits.

Hill dedicated himself to this exploration for the next twenty years, and in 1928 he published his findings in a series of sixteen pamphlets called *The Law of Success*. This work became the basis for everything that followed in Hill's career, including his landmark *Think and Grow Rich* in 1937.

That later volume is primarily a digest and refinement of insights Hill first set down in *The Law of Success*. But some of Hill's most valuable ideas didn't make it into *Think and Grow Rich*. Hill's chapter here on "The

Golden Rule" is one of his clearest and most poignant statements on how your thoughts directly shape your experience. Likewise, his chapters on "Self-Control," "Accurate Thought," and "Concentration" highlight some of his sharpest insights.

The Law of Success remains Hill's most ambitious and wide-ranging exploration of the principles upon which greatness is built. This condensed edition retains all of the core points and strategies of Hill's original work.

While technology has obviously undergone radical changes since Hill published this book, his insights into human nature and the ingredients of achievement remain strikingly relevant.

If you are pursuing any personally meaningful aim—whether launching a business, attaining distinction as an artist or professional, or repairing injustice in the world—this book may prove one of the most significant learning experiences of your life. Return to it several times; memorize its lessons; and, above all, *use it.*

—Mitch Horowitz

The Master Mind

This is a course in the fundamentals of success. Success is largely a matter of adapting to the changing circumstances of life in a spirit of harmony and poise. Harmony is based on understanding the forces around you. This course analyzes those forces and provides a blueprint to success.

To begin with, *you can never exercise power and attain success without the type of personality that influences others to willingly cooperate with you.* Each lesson teaches you how to build a winning personality through the fifteen laws of success. They are:

1. **A DEFINITE CHIEF AIM**
2. **SELF-CONFIDENCE**
3. **THE HABIT OF SAVING**
4. **INITIATIVE AND LEADERSHIP**
5. **IMAGINATION**

6. ENTHUSIASM

7. SELF-CONTROL

8. THE HABIT OF DOING MORE THAN PAID FOR

9. PLEASING PERSONALITY

10. ACCURATE THOUGHT

11. CONCENTRATION

12. COOPERATION

13. PROFITING BY FAILURE

14. TOLERANCE

15. THE GOLDEN RULE

The surest way to advance quickly through these principles, and into the fullness of your success, is with the aid of a Master Mind group. A Master Mind group consists of several people who coordinate their minds in pursuit of a goal.

The group may consist of any number from two or higher. Select the members of your Master Mind group carefully—the key ingredient is harmony and cooperation. You may focus on one group goal, or each member may have his own personal aims. Arrange a time to meet regularly to discuss your plans and ideas, and to exchange advice and guidance. When you're not together, hold each member's wishes and needs in your mind.

This friendly alliance, if carried out with purpose and harmony, will, in time, yield extraordinary results. For example, everyone in the group gains the ability to gather insight through the subconscious minds of all the other members. This produces a more vivid imaginative and mental state in which new ideas "flash" into your awareness.

Every high achiever I know has employed the power of the Master Mind. Do not neglect it.

A Definite Chief Aim

Probably ninety-five percent of all people drift aimlessly through life, without the slightest conception of the work for which they are best fitted, or even the need for a *definite* objective toward which to strive.

A person's acts are always in harmony with his dominating thoughts. Any *definite chief aim* that is deliberately fixed in the mind, with the determination to realize it, eventually saturates the subconscious until it influences all aspects of one's being.

Your *definite chief aim* should be selected with deliberate care. And after you select it you should write it out and place it where you will see it when you wake in the morning and retire at night. You must write down your aim—it is the first step towards its actualization.

You can impress your *definite chief aim* upon your subconscious through the principle called *autosuggestion*. In the simplest terms this is a suggestion that you make to yourself consistently and with deep feeling. Be certain that your *definite purpose* is constructive; that its attainment will bring hardship and misery to none; that it will bring you and your loved ones peace and prosperity; then apply the principle of self-suggestion, holding this idea constantly in your mind.

The subconscious is like a magnet, and when it has been vitalized and thoroughly saturated with any *definite purpose* it has a tendency to attract all that is necessary for the attainment of that purpose—in ideas, resources, circumstances, and people.

There is some *one thing* that you can do better than anyone else. Search until you find that particular line of endeavor, and make it your *definite chief aim*. Then direct all of your forces toward it with the belief that you are going to win. You will most likely attain the greatest success by finding what work you like best, for you generally succeed when you can thrown your whole heart and soul into something.

To be sure of success, your *definite chief aim* should be backed with a *burning desire* for its achievement. Merely desiring freedom would never release a man from prison if it were not sufficiently strong to cause him to do something to entitle himself to freedom.

You must experience your desire with a heartfelt passion. *Singleness of purpose* is essential for success.

Self-Confidence

You are now at one of the most unusual chapters in this book—because it consists largely of a *personal pledge*. I want you to consider this pledge very carefully, and then write it down and sign your name to it.

Repeat this pledge at least once a day until it has become a part of your mental makeup. Keep a copy of it before you as a daily remainder. By doing so you will again be making use of *autosuggestion*—or self-suggestion—to develop the crucial trait of self-confidence.

Never mind what anyone may say about your method. Outside your Master Mind group, you don't have to talk to anyone about it. In fact, it's probably best not to. Just remember that it is your business to succeed, and this creed, if mastered and applied, will take you a long way.

I believe in myself. I believe in my coworkers. I believe in my employer. I believe in my friends. I believe in my family. I believe that God will lend me everything I need to succeed if I do my best to earn it through faithful and honest service. I believe in prayer and will never close my eyes in sleep without praying for divine guidance to be patient with others and tolerant of those who do not believe as I do. I believe that success is the result of intellectual effort and does not depend upon blind luck or sharp-practices or double-crossing. I believe that I will get from life what I put into it, therefore I will conduct myself toward others as I would want them to act toward me. I will not spread or listen to slander and gossip. I will not slight my work no matter what I may see others doing. I will render the best service possible because I have pledged myself to succeed in life, and I know that true success is the result of conscientious and efficient effort. Finally, I will forgive those who offend me because I realize that I shall sometimes offend others and I will need their forgiveness.

Remember: Write this statement out, sign it, recite it daily, and keep it where you can see it.

The Habit of Saving

Saving money is a matter of habit. For this reason, we begin with a brief analysis of the *law of habit*.

The law of habit shapes your personality. Through repetition any act becomes a habit, and the mind may sometimes seem to be nothing more than a mass of motivating forces growing from our daily habits.

Here is how to develop the immensely valuable habit of saving:

FIRST

Through your *definite chief aim* set up in your mind an accurate and detailed description of what you want, including the amount of money you intend to earn. Your subconscious takes over this picture and uses it as a blueprint to mold your thoughts and actions into *practical plans*. Through the law of habit you keep the object of your *definite chief aim* fixed in your mind until it becomes firmly and permanently implanted there. This practice will erode the poverty consciousness and set up a prosperity consciousness. You will actually begin to DEMAND prosperity; you will begin to expect it; you will begin to prepare yourself to receive it and to use it wisely, thus paving the way for the *habit of saving*.

SECOND
Having in this manner increased your earning ability you make further use of the law of habit by committing, in the written statement of your *definite chief aim*, to save a fixed percentage of all that you earn. As your earnings increase, your savings increase in proportion, and you will be on the road to financial stability.

Initiative and Leadership

eadership is essential for attaining success—and *initiative* is the foundation upon which *leadership* sits.

Initiative is that exceedingly rare quality that impels a person to do what ought to be done *without being told to*. Leadership is found only among those who have acquired the *habit of initiative*.

Leadership is something you must invite yourself into; it will never thrust itself upon you. If you carefully analyze all the leaders with which you are familiar, you will see that they not only exercised *initiative*, but also went about their work with a *definite purpose*. You will further see that they possessed *self-confidence*. Anyone who lacks these traits is not really a leader.

Here is the exact procedure to become a person of *initiative* and *leadership*:

FIRST

You must eliminate all *procrastination*. This habit gnaws at the soul. Nothing is possible until you throw it off.

SECOND

You can best develop *initiative* by making it your business to interest those around you in doing the same. You learn best that which you teach.

THIRD

Understand that there are two kinds of *leadership*. One is as deadly as the other is helpful. The deadly brand belongs to pseudo-leaders who *force* their will on others. The brand we are after was seen in Abraham Lincoln: his leadership brought truth, justice, and understanding. Those qualities have engraved his name upon the heart of the world. Emulate them.

Imagination

You will never have a *definite purpose* in life, you will never have *self-confidence*, you will never have *initiative* and *leadership*, unless you first create these qualities in your *imagination* and see them as yours.

You may see how important *imagination* is when you stop to realize that it is the only thing in the world over which you have absolute control. Others may cheat you or deprive you of material wealth, but no one can deny you the control and use of your *imagination*.

Your imagination is the mirror of your soul, and you have every right to stand before that mirror and see yourself as you wish to be. You have *the right* to see in that mirror the mansion you intend to own, the business you plan to manage, the station in life you intend to occupy. *Your imagination belongs to you.* Use it! The more you use it the more efficiently it will serve you.

Your battle for achievement is already half won when *you know definitely what you want.*

The selection of your *definite chief aim* calls for both imagination and *decision.* The power of decision also grows with use. Prompt decision in compelling the *imagination* to create a *definite chief aim* gives you a more powerful capacity to reach decisions in other matters.

Enthusiasm

nthusiasm is a state of mind that inspires you to *action*. But it does more—it is contagious, and it arouses everyone around you.

Enthusiasm is the vital force of life. The greatest leaders know how to instill enthusiasm in their followers. Enthusiasm is the most important factor in salesmanship. It is by far the most crucial factor in public speaking.

Mix enthusiasm with your work and it will seem neither hard nor monotonous. *Enthusiasm* will so energize your body that you can get along with less than half the usual amount of sleep and perform two to three times as much work as usual, without fatigue.

Enthusiasm is no mere figure of speech; it is a *vital force* through which you can recharge your body and develop a dynamic personality. Some are blessed with natural enthusiasm; others must acquire it. The procedure through which it may be developed is simple. It begins by doing the work that you like best. If you cannot, for the time being, engage in such work that is all more reason to adopt a *definite chief aim*, and you will begin to move toward it.

Lack of money and many other circumstances may force you to engage in work that you do not like. But no one can stop you from determining your *definite chief aim*; nor can anyone stop you from planning ways and means for translating that aim into reality; nor can anyone stop you from mixing *enthusiasm* with your plans.

When you are enthusiastic over your goods or services, or the speech you are delivering, your mental state becomes obvious to all who hear you. The tone with which you make a statement, more than the statement itself, carries conviction or fails to convince. Words are devitalized sounds unless colored with enthusiasm.

But take note: *Never express, through words or acts, something that does not harmonize with your beliefs—or you will lose the ability to influence others.*

I do not believe that I can afford to deceive anyone about anything; but *I know that I cannot afford to deceive myself.* To do so would destroy the power of my pen. It is only when I write with the *fire of enthusiasm* that my writing impresses others. *It is only when I speak from a heart that is bursting with belief in my message* that I can move my audience to accept it.

LAW SEVEN

Self-Control

Self-control is the force through which you direct your enthusiasm to constructive ends. Without self-control enthusiasm resembles unharnessed lightening—it may strike anywhere, destroying life and property. The balanced person possesses both *enthusiasm* and *self-control*.

The majority of our griefs result from lack of self-control. Scripture is full of injunctions to *self-control*. It even urges us to love our enemies and to forgive those who injure us. The law of non-resistance runs like a golden cord throughout the Bible.

Where does *self-control* come from? Consider this very carefully: *Thought* is the only thing over which you have total dominion. This is of profound significance. It suggests that *thought* is your nearest approach to Divinity on this earthly plane. This fact carries another vital idea: namely, that *thought* is your most important tool; the one with which you may shape your destiny. Divine Providence did not make *thought* the sole power over which you have absolute control without associating that power with potentialities which, if understood and developed, would strain belief.

Self-control is solely a matter of thought-control.

You are searching for the magic key to power; and yet you have the key in your hands, and may use it the moment you learn to *control your thoughts.*

A student once asked how he could control his thoughts in a state of intense anger. I replied, *"In exactly the same way that you would change your manner and tone if you were in a heated argument with a family member and heard the doorbell ring, signaling that company was about to visit. You would control yourself because you would desire to."*

If you have ever faced a similar predicament, where you found it necessary to quickly conceal your feelings and change your facial expression, you know that it can be done *because you WANT TO!*

Back of all achievement, back of all *self-control*, back of all *thought control*, is that magic something called DESIRE! It is no exaggeration to say that you are limited only by the depth of your *desire.*

When your *desire* is strong enough you will appear to possess superhuman abilities. No one has ever explained this phenomenon of the mind, and perhaps no one ever will, but if you doubt that it exists you have only to experiment.

Don't say, "It can't be done," or that you are different from the thousands of people who have achieved noteworthy success. If you are "different" it is only because *they desired the object of their achievement with greater depth and intensity than you.*

The energy that most people dissipate through lack of self-control, or fritter away gossiping, would, if controlled and directed constructively, be sufficient to attain their *definite chief aim,* provided they have one.

The Habit of Doing More Than Paid For

Here is one of the most important laws of this philosophy: *A person is most efficient, and will more quickly and easily succeed, when engaged in work that he loves, or work that he performs for someone he loves.*

When the element of love enters any task, the quality of the work improves and the quantity increases. When engaged in work that you love it is no hardship to do more and better work than you are paid for; for this very reason you owe it to yourself to find the work you like best.

There are many reasons to do more than you are paid for, but two stand out:

FIRST

By establishing a reputation as someone who performs more and better work than paid for, you benefit by comparison with competitors who rarely show such commitment.

SECOND

Suppose that you want to develop a strong right arm. You could develop such an arm *only by giving it the hardest use*. Out of resistance comes strength. By performing more and better service than paid for, you not only develop your skill and ability but also can *command* greater remuneration than the majority who do not perform such service.

Try this experiment: For the next six months commit to rendering useful service to at least one person every day, for which *you neither expect nor accept monetary pay*. Go at this experiment with faith that it will prove to you one of the most powerful laws of success: that you succeed best and quickest by helping others to succeed.

Pleasing Personality

Your personality is the sum total of your characteristics and appearance. The clothes you wear, the lines in your face, the vitality of your body, your handshake, your tone of voice, the thoughts you think, the character you have developed by those thoughts—all are parts of your *personality*.

Whether your personality is attractive is another matter.

By far the most important part of your personality is your *character*, and is therefore the part that is not visible. The style of your clothes and their appropriateness also constitute an important part of your personality, for it is true that people derive first impressions from your outward appearance.

There is one way to express your personality that will *always attract*: *taking a heartfelt interest in others*.

Study people closely enough to find something about them or their work that you *truly* admire. Talk to them about it. Show genuine interest in it. Only in this way can you develop a personality that will be irresistibly *attractive*.

Cheap flattery has the opposite effect. It repels instead of attracting. It is so shallow that even the ignorant easily detect it.

As noted, *character* is the most important factor in *personality*. How can you build *character*? Follow these steps:

FIRST
Identify people whose characters have the qualities you wish to emulate, and develop these qualities through *autosuggestion*.

SECOND
Let the dominating thought of your mind be a picture of the person that you are *deliberately building*.

THIRD
Find at least one person each day, and more if possible, in whom you see some good quality and *praise it*. But remember, this praise must be *genuine* and not insincere flattery.

I cannot over-emphasize the benefits of praising, openly and enthusiastically, the good qualities in others; for this habit will soon reward you with a feeling of self-respect and manifestation of gratitude from others, which will modify your entire personality.

Accurate Thought

You cannot succeed without *accurate thought*. *Accurate thought* involves two fundamentals. First, you must separate *facts* from mere *information*. Much "information" is not based upon facts. Second, you must divide *facts* into two classes: *important* and *unimportant*.

All facts that *aid* your pursuit of your *definite chief aim* (without violating the rights of others) are *important* and *relevant*. All that you cannot use are the opposite. If you direct your attention exclusively to the *important facts*—those that contribute to the realization of your aim—you will attain a special clarity.

You must also avoid the vulgar and self-destructive habit of spreading and listening to gossip. If you permit yourself to be swayed by all manner of information—especially rumors and gossip—you will never become an *accurate thinker*, and you will not attain your *definite chief aim*.

We will now explore a special form of *thought* that does much more than gather and organize facts. In many ways, this form of thought is the keynote of this course. We will call it *creative thought*. With a few exceptions man has not yet recognized *creative thought* as the connecting link to the power of *infinite intelligence*.

To understand how this occurs we return to the topic of *autosuggestion*. The sense impressions arising from your environment, or from the statements and actions of others, are mere ordinary suggestions; but the sense impressions that *you place in your own mind*—that you deliberately and confidently dwell upon, think of at every opportunity, and mentally picture and *feel*—are the product of self-suggestion, or *autosuggestion*.

Autosuggestion is the telegraph line over which you register in your subconscious the aim you wish to *create* in physical form.

The subconscious is the intermediary between the conscious *thinking mind* and *infinite intelligence*. You can invoke the aid of *infinite intelligence* through the *subconscious* only by giving it clear instructions as to what you want. Hence the critical need for a *definite chief aim*.

The subconscious records the suggestions that you send it through autosuggestion, and invokes the aid of infinite intelligence in translating these suggestions into their natural physical form, through natural means which are in no way out of the ordinary.

First, you must select the picture to be recorded (your *definite chief aim*). Then you fix your conscious mind upon this purpose with such intensity that it communicates with the subconscious through autosuggestion, and registers that picture. You then watch for and expect manifestations of the physical realization of that picture.

Bear in mind that you do not sit down and wait, nor go to sleep, with the expectation that *infinite intelligence* has granted your desire. No, you go right ahead doing your daily work *with full faith and confidence that natural ways and means for the attainment of your definite purpose will open to you at the proper time and in a suitable manner.*

Infinite intelligence will not build you a home and deliver it ready to enter. But *infinite intelligence* will open the way and provide the necessary means, including insights, intuitions, and ideas, which allow you to build your own house. Do not reply upon miracles for your *definite chief aim*; rely upon the power of *infinite intelligence* to guide you, through natural channels and laws, to its attainment.

Concentration

To move safely and accurately toward a target you must *concentrate* on it. Two important laws enter into the act of *concentrating* on a given desire. One is the law of autosuggestion, which we have already reviewed; the other is the law of habit, which we will now consider in further detail.

Habit grows from environment and repetition— from doing and thinking the same thing over and over. Except for rare occasions when the mind rises above environment, we draw the material out of which *thought* is created from our surroundings, and *habit* crystalizes this thought into a permanent fixture.

To attain success, you must develop habits that lead toward constructive thoughts and actions in the direction of your *definite chief aim*. Follow this procedure to acquire the habits you need:

FIRST

At the beginning of the formation of a new habit put force and enthusiasm into your expression. *Feel what you think.* Remember that you are taking the first steps toward making a new mental path; it is much harder at first than it will be later. Make the path as clear and as deep as you can at the beginning, so that you can readily see it the next time you wish to follow it.

SECOND

Keep your attention firmly *concentrated* on the new path you are building, and keep you mind far away from the old paths.

THIRD

Travel over your newly made paths as often as possible. Make opportunities for doing so. The more you traverse these new paths the sooner they will become familiar and easily travelled.

FOURTH

Resist the temptation to travel over the older, easier paths that you have used in the past. Every time you resist a temptation, you grow stronger.

FIFTH

Be sure that you have mapped out the right path as your *definite chief aim*—and then charge at it without fear or doubt.

Cooperation

Success cannot be attained singlehandedly. It requires *cooperative effort*. Even a hermit in the wilderness is *dependent* upon forces outside himself for existence. The more he becomes a part of civilization, the more he *depends* upon *cooperative effort*.

If your philosophy is based upon cooperation instead of competition you will not only acquire the necessities and luxuries of life with less effort, but you will enjoy an additional reward in *happiness*. Fortunes acquired through cooperative effort inflict no scars upon the hearts of their owners.

Ordinary cooperative effort produces power. But cooperative effort that is based upon complete harmony of purpose develops *superpower*. Gave a person of average ability a sufficiently visualized and passionately felt motive and he will develop superpower. Men work harder for *an ideal* than they will for money. Remember this when searching for a motive to develop group cooperation.

Men generally respond to three major motivating forces:

1. The motive of self-preservation.
2. The motive of sexual contact.
3. The motive of financial and social power.

Regardless of who you are, or your *definite chief aim*, if you depend upon others—as almost all of us do—you must present them with a motive strong enough to ensure their full cooperation.

Profiting by Failure

What we typically call *failure* is, in reality, *temporary defeat.* Moreover, this temporary defeat often proves a blessing, for it jolts us and redirects our energies along different and more desirable paths.

Sound character is usually the outcome of reverses, setbacks, and temporary defeat.

Neither temporary defeat nor adversity spell failure to one who looks upon such things as a teacher. A great and lasting lesson appears in every reverse and defeat—and, usually, it could be learned in no other way.

Ralph Waldo Emerson explored this principle in his great essay "Compensation." If you haven't read it, do so—and reread it every three months.

I used to *hate* my enemies. But this was before I learned how well they were serving me by keeping me everlastingly on the alert, lest some weak spot in my character provide an opening through which I might be damaged. Enemies discover your defects and point them out; friends, even if they see them, say nothing.

I am convinced that failure is Nature's plan through which she hurdle-jumps men of destiny and prepares them to do their work. Failure is Nature's great crucible in which she burns the dross from the human heart and purifies the metal of a man so that it can stand the test of hard usage.

Tolerance

Always remember these two facts about *intolerance*.

FIRST

Intolerance makes enemies; it disintegrates the organized forces of society; it dethrones reason and substitutes mob psychology in its place. *Intolerance* is a form of ignorance that must be mastered before enduring success may be attained.

SECOND

Intolerance is the chief disintegrating force in the organized religions of the world, where it plays havoc with the greatest power for good on earth by breaking it up into small sects, which spend as much time opposing each other as in combating evil.

Anything that impedes the progress of civilization also stands as a barrier to each individual.

I once encountered intolerance in myself, and I vowed to *unlearn much that I had previously considered the truth.* I discovered that I had acquired my views of religion, politics, economics, and many other important subjects simply by "picking up" what my family believed.

Most of my views were unsupported by even a reasonable hypothesis, much less facts. Imagine suddenly discovering that most of your philosophy had been built on bias and prejudice.

I urge you to learn how and where you acquired your philosophy of life in order to trace your prejudices and biases to their original source—and to discover, as I did, the degree to which you are the result of training you received before the age of fifteen.

The Golden Rule

For more than twenty-five years I have been observing how men behave in positions of power, and I have seen that the man who attains power in any way other than a slow, step-by-step process is in constant danger of destroying himself and all whom he influences.

For more than four thousand years humanity has preached the Golden Rule as the foundation of good conduct. But the world has accepted the letter while totally missing the spirit of this universal injunction. We acknowledge the Golden Rule merely as a sound principle—but we have failed to understand the *inner law* upon which it is based.

The Golden Rule means to do unto others as you would wish them to do unto you. But why? What is the *real* reason for this kindly consideration of others?

The reason is this: There is an eternal law by which we reap what we sow. When you select the rule of conduct by which to guide your life, you are more likely be fair and just if you *know* that you are setting into motion a *power* that will run its course in the lives of others, returning, finally, to help or hinder you, according to its nature.

It is your choice to deal unjustly with others, but if you understand the law upon which the Golden Rule is based, you must know that your unjust deals will return to you.

You cannot pervert or change the course of this law—*but you can adapt yourself to its nature and thereby use it as an irresistible power that will carry you to heights of achievement.*

This law does not stop merely by flinging back at you your *acts* of injustice and unkindness; it goes further—much further—and *returns to you the results of every thought that you release.*

Therefore, it is advisable not only to "do unto others as you wish them to do unto you." But to make full use of this great Universal Law you must "*think of others as you wish them to think of you.*" The law upon which the Golden Rule is based begins affecting you, for good or evil, the moment you release a *thought.*

Understand this law and you understand *all* that the Bible has to reveal. The Bible presents one unbroken chain of evidence that man is the maker of his own destiny.

All your *acts* toward others, and even your *thoughts* of others, are registered in your subconscious through the principle of autosuggestion, thereby building your own character in exact duplicate. Can you see how important it is to guard those acts and thoughts?

You cannot act toward another without having first created the nature of that act in your own *thought, and you cannot release a thought without planting the sum and substance of it in your own subconscious, there to become a part of your character.*

Grasp this simple principle and you will understand why you cannot afford to hate or envy another person. You will also understand why you cannot afford to strike back at those who do you an injustice. Likewise, you will understand the injunction, "Return good for evil."

Throughout this course I have emphasized one particular principle for the purpose of revealing that your personality is the sum total of your *thoughts* and *acts*—and that you come to resemble the nature of your dominating *thoughts*.

Man, alone, has the power to transform his *thoughts* into physical reality. Use the palace of your mind methodically, carefully, and deliberately—and you will reconstruct on the outside those dreams that dwell within.

NAPOLEON HILL was born in 1883 in Wise County, Virginia. He was employed as a secretary, a reporter, the manager of a coalmine and a lumberyard, and attended law school, before he began working as a journalist for *Bob Taylor's Magazine,* an inspirational and general-interest journal. In 1908 the job led to his interviewing steel magnate Andrew Carnegie. The encounter changed the course of Hill's life. Carnegie believed success could be distilled into definite principles that anyone could follow. He urged Hill to interview the greatest industrialists, financiers, and inventors of the era to discover these principles. Hill pursued the challenge for twenty years, resulting in his landmark volume *The Law of Success* in 1928. The sixteen-volume work formed the basis for Hill's worldwide sensation *Think and Grow Rich* in 1937. Hill dedicated the rest of his life to documenting and refining the principles of success. The motivational pioneer died in 1970 in South Carolina.

MITCH HOROWITZ, who abridged and introduced this volume, is the PEN Award-winning author of books including *Occult America* and *The Miracle Club: How*

Thoughts Become Reality. *The Washington Post* says Mitch "treats esoteric ideas and movements with an even-handed intellectual studiousness that is too often lost in today's raised-voice discussions." Follow him @MitchHorowitz.

THE MASTER
KEY TO RICHES

THE MASTER
KEY TO RICHES

by Napoleon Hill

The Secrets to Wealth,
Power, and Achievement
from the Author of
Think and Grow Rich

Abridged and Introduced
by Mitch Horowitz

THE CONDENSED CLASSICS LIBRARY™

Contents

The Secrets to Power

This is probably the most unusual book Napoleon Hill ever wrote. He dramatically presents its text as a speech delivered by a "masked rich man," who decides to share his wealth secrets with the world. In using this device, Hill was borrowing a theme that has long been popular in America's alternative spiritual culture—placing lessons in the mouth of a mysterious master, who may be real, invented, or a mixture of both.

Hill's unknown speaker is basically a personification of the voice of practical wisdom that ran through all of his books. In *The Master Key to Riches*, the speaker captures the essentials of Hill's ideas and adds some additional insights that came to Hill when he published this book in 1945, toward the victorious end of World War II, with America's Great Depression finally a memory and his classic work, *Think and Grow Rich*, eight years behind him.

As with all of Hill's books, you can more or less glean the totality of his philosophy from this one, in which he states his seventeen principles of success, along with other lists and testaments that guide you through towards effectiveness, attainment, and achievement. *The Master Key to Riches* is notable in that it probably features more lists and bulleted points than ever before, and in a pleasingly compressed form so that the book serves as an introduction to the newcomer and a refresher to the veteran. In my view, a reader always benefits from a review of Hill's ideas, as each reading reveals something new or previously overlooked. That has been my personal experience.

Another important aspect of this book is that it features what I consider Hill's clearest and most sustained explanation of the power of the "applied faith." I have sometimes struggled with the idea of faith in Hill's program. Chapter eight, "Applied Faith," has proven especially helpful to me in that regard, and I direct you to pay close attention to it.

I now turn you over to the voice of Hill's "Masked Rich Man from Happy Valley," whose revelations and insights are the closest thing we have, and likely ever will, to a science of success.

—Mitch Horowitz

Think!

Many centuries ago a very wealthy and wise philosopher by the name of Croesus, an adviser to Cyrus, King of the Persians, said:

I am reminded, O King: and take this lesson to heart; that there is a Wheel on which the affairs of men revolve, and its mechanism is such that it prevents any man from being always fortunate.

The Master Key to Riches was designed for the purpose of aiding men in the mastery and control of this great Wheel, to the end that it may be made to yield them an abundance of all that they desire, including the Twelve Great Riches of Life described in the second chapter.

Remember, you who are beginning the study of this philosophy, that this same Wheel that "prevents any man from being always fortunate" may provide also that no man shall be always unfortunate, provided he will take possession of his own mind and direct it to the attain of some Definite Major Purpose in life.

CHAPTER ONE

The Beginning of All Riches

The largest audience ever assembled in the history of mankind sat breathlessly awaiting the message of a mysterious man who was about to reveal to the world the secret of his riches.

Slowly the curtain began to rise. The speaker walked briskly to the podium. He was dressed in a long black robe and wore a mask over his eyes. His hair was grayish, and he appeared about sixty years of age.

He stood silently for a few moments, while the cameras flashed. Then, speaking slowly, in a voice soft and pleasing, like music, be began his message:

You have come here to seek the MASTER KEY TO RICHES!

You have come because of that human urge for the better things in life, which is the common desire of all people.

You desire economic security, which money alone can provide.

Some of you desire an outlet for your talents in order that you may have the joy of creating your own riches.

Some of you are seeking the easy way to riches, with the hope that you will find it without giving anything in return; that too is a common desire. But it is a desire I shall hope to modify for your benefit, as from experience I have learned that there is no such thing as something for noting.

There is but one sure way to riches, and it may be attained only by those who have the MASTER KEY TO RICHES!

The MASTER KEY is an ingenious device with which those who possess it may unlock the door to the solution all of their problems. Its powers of magic transcend those of the famous Aladdin's Lamp.

It opens the door to sound health.

It opens the door to love and romance.

It opens the door to friendship, by revealing the traits of personality and character that make enduring friends.

It reveals the method by which every adversity, every failure, every disappointment, every mistaken error of judgment, and every past defeat may be transmuted into riches of a priceless value.

It kindles anew the dead hopes of all who possess it, and it reveals the formula by which one may "tune in" and draw upon the great reservoir of Infinite Intelligence, through that state of mind known as Faith.

It opens the doors, one by one, to the Twelve Great Riches of Life, which I shall presently describe for you in detail.

Listen carefully to what I have to say, for I shall not pass this way again. Listen not only with open ears, but also with open minds and eager hearts, remembering that no man may hear that for which he has not the preparation for hearing.

Before I describe the Twelve Great Riches let me reveal to you some of the riches you already possess; riches of which most of you may not be conscious.

First, I would have you recognize that each of you is a plural personality, although you may regard yourself as a single personality. You and every other person consist of least two distinct personalities, and many of you possess more.

One is your "other self," a positive sort of person who thinks in terms of opulence, sound health, love and friendship, personal achievement, creative vision, service to others, and who guides you unerringly to the attainment of all of these blessings. It is this self which alone is capable of recognizing and approaching the

Twelve Great Riches. This is not an imaginary personality of which I speak. It is real.

When your negative personality is in control your radio station picks up only the negative thought vibrations that are being sent out by hundreds of millions of other negative personalities throughout the world. These are accepted, acted upon, and translated into their physical equivalent in terms of the circumstances of life that you do not wish.

When your positive personality is in control it picks up only the positive thought vibrations being released by millions of other positive personalities throughout the world, and translates them into their physical equivalent in terms of prosperity, sound health, love, hope, faith, peace of mind and happiness; the values of life for which you and every other normal person are searching.

I have come to reveal to you the Master Key by which you may attain these and many other riches. That mysterious key that unlocks the doors to the solution of all human problems, acquires all riches, and places every individual thought pattern under the control of one's "other self."

When I speak of "riches" I have in mind the greater riches whose possessors have made life pay off on their own terms—the terms of full and complete happiness. I call these the "Twelve Riches of Life." And I sincerely wish to share them with all of you who are prepared to receive them, in whole or in part.

You may wonder about my willingness to share, so I shall tell you that the MASTER KEY TO RICHES enables its possessors to add to their own store of riches everything of value when they share with others. This is one of the strangest facts of life, but it is a fact which each of you must recognize and respect. Now let us pass onto the description of the Twelve Riches.

CHAPTER TWO

The Twelve Riches of Life

The greatest of all riches is . . .

1. **A Positive Mental Attitude.** All riches of whatever nature, begin as a state of mind; and let us
remember that a state of mind is the one and only
thing over which any person has complete, unchal-
lenged right of control. It is highly significant that
the Creator provided man with control over nothing except the power to shape his own thoughts
and the privilege of fitting them to any pattern of
his choice. Mental attitude is important because
it converts the brain into the equivalent of an
electro-magnet, which attracts one's dominating
thoughts, aims, and purposes. It also attracts one's
fears, worries, and doubts. A positive mental atti-

tude is the starting point of all riches, whether they are riches of a material nature or intangible wishes. It attracts the wishes of a true friendship. And the riches one finds in the hope of future achievement.

2. **Sound Physical Health.** Sound health begins with a "health consciousness" produced by a mind that thinks in terms of health and not in terms of illness, plus temperance of habits in eating and properly balancing physical activities.

3. **Harmony in Human Relationships.** Harmony with others begins with one's self, for it is true, as Shakespeare said, and there are benefits available to those who comply with his admonitions, "To thine own self be true, and it must follow, as the night the day, thou cans't not then be false to any man."

4. **Freedom from Fear.** No man who fears anything is a free man! Fear is a harbinger of evil, and wherever it appears one may find a cause that must be eliminated before he may become rich in the fuller sense. The seven basic fears that appear most often in the mind of men are: (1) fear of POVERTY, (2) fear of CRITICISM, (3) fear of ILL HEALTH, (4) fear of LOSS OF LIFE, (5) fear of LOSS OF LIBERTY, (6) fear of OLD AGE, (7) fear of DEATH.

5. **The Hope of Achievement.** The greatest of all forms of happiness comes as a result of the hope

of achievement of some yet unattained desire; and poor beyond description is the person who cannot look to the future with hope that he will become the person he would like to be, or with the belief that he will attain the objective he has failed to reach in the past.

6. **The Capacity for Faith.** Faith is the connecting link between the conscious mind of the man and the great universal reservoir of Infinite Intelligence. It is the fertile soil of the garden of the human mind wherein may be produced all of the riches of life. It is the "eternal elixir" that gives creative power and action to the impulses of thought. Faith is the basis of so-called miracles, and of many mysteries that cannot be explained by the rules of logic or science. Faith is the "spiritual chemical" that, when it is mixed with prayer, gives one direct and immediate connection with Infinite Intelligence. Faith is the power that transmutes the ordinary energies of thought into their spiritual equivalent. And it is the one power through which the Cosmic Force of Infinite Intelligence may be appropriated to the uses of man.

7. **Willingness to Share One's Blessings.** He who has not learned the blessed art of sharing has not learned the true path to happiness, for happiness

comes only by sharing. And let it be forever remembered that all riches may be embellished and multiplied by the simple process of sharing them where they may serve others. And let it be also remembered that the space one occupies in the hearts of his fellowmen is determined precisely by the service he renders through some form of sharing his blessings.

8. **A Labor of Love.** There can be no richer man than he who has found a labor of love and who is busily engaged in performing it, for labor is the highest form of human expression of desire. Labor is the liaison between the demand and the supply of all human needs, the forerunner of all human progress, the medium by which the imagination of man is given the wings of action. And all labor of love is sanctified because it brings the joy of self-expression to him who performs it.

9. **An Open Mind on all Subjects.** Tolerance, which is among the higher attributes of culture, is expressed only by those who hold an open mind on all subjects at all times. And it is only the man with an open mind who becomes truly educated and who is thus prepared to avail himself of the greater riches of life.

10. **Self-discipline.** The man who is not master of

himself may never become the master of anything. He who is the master of self may become the master of his own earthly destiny, the "master of fate, the Captain of his soul." And the highest form of self-discipline consists in the expression of the humility of the heart when one has attained great riches or has been overtaken by that which is commonly called "success."

11. **The Capacity to Understand People.** The man who is rich in the understanding of people always recognizes that all people are fundamentally alike in that they have evolved from the same stem; that all human activities are inspired by one or more of the nine basic motives of life: (1) the emotion of LOVE, (2) the emotion of SEX, (3) the desire for MATERIAL GAIN, (4) the desire for SELF PRESERVATION (5) the desire for FREEDOM OF BODY AND MIND, (6) the desire for SELF-EXPRESSION, (7) the desire for perpetuation of LIFE AFTER DEATH, (8) the emotion of ANGER, and (9) the emotion of FEAR. And the man who would understand others must first understand himself.

12. **Economic Security.** The last, though not least in importance, is the tangible portion of the "Twelve Riches." Economic security is not attained by pos-

session of money alone. It is attained by the service one renders, for useful service may be converted into all forms of human needs, with or without the use of money.

Presently I shall acquaint you with the principles by which money and all other forms of riches may be obtained, but first you must be prepared to make application of these principles. Your mind must be conditioned for the acceptance of riches just as the soil of the earth must be prepared for the planting of seeds.

When one is ready for a thing it is sure to appear!

This does not mean the things one may need will appear without a cause, for there is a vast difference between one's "*needs*" and one's *readiness* to receive. To miss this distinction is to miss the major benefits I shall endeavor to convey. So let me lead you into *readiness* to receive the riches that you desire.

CHAPTER THREE

The Eight Princes

My riches came through the aid of others. Some of these helpers have been well known. Some have been strangers whose names you will not recognize. Among these *strangers* are eight of my friends who have done most for me in preparing my mind for the acceptance of riches. I call them the "Eight Princes." They serve me when I am awake and they serve me when I am asleep.

The Princes serve me through a technique that is simple and adaptable. Every night, as the last order of the day's activities, the Princes and I have a roundtable session, the major purpose of which is to permit me to express my gratitude for the service they have rendered me during the day. My Princes of Guidance are:

1. PRINCE OF MATERIAL PROSPERITY, I am grateful to you for having kept my mind attuned to

the consciousness of opulence and plenty, and free from the fear of poverty and want.

2. PRINCE OF SOUND PHYSICAL HEALTH, I am grateful to you for having attuned my mind to the consciousness of sound health, thereby providing the means by which every cell of my body and every physical organ is being adequately supplied with an inflow of cosmic energy sufficient unto its needs, and providing a direct contact with Infinite Intelligence which is sufficient for the distribution and application of this energy where it is required.

3. PRINCE OF PEACE OF MIND, I am grateful to you for having kept my mind free from all inhibitions and self-imposed limitations, thereby providing my body and my mind with complete rest.

4. PRINCE OF HOPE, I am grateful to you for the fulfillment of today's desires, and for your promise of fulfillment of tomorrow's aims.

5. PRINCE OF FAITH, I am grateful to you for the guidance which you have given me; for your having inspired me to do that which has been helpful to me, and for turning me back from doing that which had it been done would have proven harmful to me. You have given power to my thoughts, momentum to my deeds, and the wisdom that has enabled me to understand the laws of Nature, and

the judgment to enable me to adapt myself to them in a spirit of harmony.

6. PRINCE OF LOVE, I am grateful to you for having inspired me to share my riches with all whom I have contacted this day; for having shown me that only that which I give away can I retain as my own. And I am grateful too for the consciousness of love with which you have endowed me, for it has made life sweet and all my relationships pleasant.

7. PRINCE OF ROMANCE, I am grateful to you for having inspired me with the spirit of youth despite the passing of the years.

8. PRINCE OF OVERALL WISDOM, my eternal gratitude to you for having transmuted into an enduring asset of priceless value, all of my past failures, defeats, errors of judgment and of deed, all fears, mistakes, disappointments, and adversities of every nature; the asset consisting of my willingness and ability to inspire others to take possession of their own minds and to use their mind-power for the attainment of the riches of life, thus providing me with the privilege of sharing all of my blessings with those who are ready to receive to them. And thereby enriching and multiplying my own blessings by the scope of their benefit to others.

Let me now share with you the following creed, so that you may adopt it as your own.

A HAPPY MAN'S CREED

I have found happiness by helping others to find it.

I have sound physical health because I live temperately in all things, and eat only the foods that Nature requires for body maintenance.

I am free from fear in all of its forms.

I hate no man, envy no man, but love all mankind.

I am engaged in a labor of love with which I mix play generously. Therefore I never grow tired.

I give thanks daily, not for more riches, but for wisdom with which to recognize, embrace, and properly use the great abundance of riches I now have at my command.

I speak no name save only to honor it.

I ask no favors of anyone except the privilege of sharing my riches with all who will receive them.

I am on good terms with my conscience. Therefore it guides me correctly in all that I do.

I have no enemies because I injure no man for any cause, but I benefit all with whom I come into contact by teaching the way to enduring riches.

I have more material wealth than I need because I am free from greed and covet only the material things I can use while I live.

I own the Estate of Happy Valley, which is not taxable because it exists mainly in my own mind in intangible riches, which cannot be assessed or appropriated except by those who adopt my way of life. I created this vast estate by observing Nature's laws and adapting my habits to conform therewith.

In the chapters that follow you fill find the MASTER KEY, which will unlock the door to this chamber and all others. And it will be in your hands when you have prepared yourself to accept it.

Chapter Four

Definiteness of Purpose

I t is impressive to recognize that all of the great leaders, in all walks of life and during all periods of history, have attained their leadership by the application of their abilities to a *definite major purpose*.

It is no less impressive to observe that those who are classified as failures have no such purpose, but they go around and around, like a ship without a rudder, coming back always empty-handed, to their starting point.

Some of these "failures" begin with a definite major purpose but they desert that purpose the moment they are overtaken by temporary defeat or strenuous opposition. They give up and quit, not knowing that there is a philosophy of success which is as dependable and as definite as the rules of mathematics, and never suspecting that temporary defeat is but a test ground which may prove a blessing in disguise if it is not accepted as final.

It is one of the great tragedies of civilization that ninety-eight of out every one hundred persons go all the way through life without coming within sight of anything that even approximates definiteness of a major purpose!

We come now to the analysis of the power of definiteness of purpose, and psychological principles from which the power is derived.

FIRST PREMISE:

The starting point of all individual achievement is the adoption of a definite purpose and a definite plan for its attainment.

SECOND PREMISE:

All achievement is the result of a motive or combination of motives, of which there are nine basic motives, which govern all voluntary actions. (We described these nine motives in chapter two.)

THIRD PREMISE:

Any dominating idea, plan or purpose held in the mind, through repetition of thought, and emotionalized with a burning desire for its realization, is taken over by the subconscious section of the mind and acted upon, and it is thus carried through to its logical climax by whatever means may be available.

FOURTH PREMISE:

Any dominating desire, plan or purpose held in the conscious mind and backed by absolute faith in its realization, is taken over and acted upon immediately by the subconscious section of the mind, *and there is no known record of this kind of a desire having ever been without fulfillment.*

FIFTH PREMISE:

The power of thought is the only thing over which any person has complete, unquestionable control—a fact so astounding that it connotes a close relationship between the mind of man and the Universal Mind of Infinite Intelligence, the connecting link between the two being FAITH.

SIXTH PREMISE:

The subconscious portion of the mind is the doorway to Infinite Intelligence, and it responds to one's demands in exactly proportion to the quality of one's FAITH! The subconscious may mind be reached through faith and given instructions as though it were a person or a complete entity unto itself.

SEVENTH PREMISE:

A definite purpose, backed by absolute faith, is a form of wisdom, and wisdom in action produces results.

The Major Advantages of Definiteness of Purpose

Definiteness of purpose develops self-reliance, personal initiative, imagination, enthusiasm, self-discipline, and concentration of effort, and all of these are prerequisites for the attainment of material success.

Definiteness of aim induces one to budget his time and to plan all his day-to-day endeavors so they lead toward the attainment of his MAJOR PURPOSE in life.

It makes one more alert in the recognition of opportunities related to the object of one's MAJOR PURPOSE, and it inspires the necessary courage to act upon those opportunities when they appear.

It inspires the cooperation of others.

It prepares the way for the full exercise of that state of mind known as FAITH, by *making the mind positive* and freeing it from the limitations of fear, doubt, and indecision.

It provides one with a *success consciousness*, without which no one may attain enduring success in any calling.

It destroys the destructive habit of procrastination.

Lastly, it leads directly to the development and the continuous maintenance of the first of the Twelve Riches, a *positive mental attitude*.

These are the major characteristics of DEFINITE-NESS OF PURPOSE, although it has many other qualities and usages, and it is directly related to each of the Twelve Riches because they are attainable only by singleness of purpose.

Definiteness of purpose can, and it should, so completely occupy the mind *that one has no time or space in the mind for thoughts of failure.*

Chapter Five

The Habit of Going the Extra Mile

An important principle of success in all walks of life and in all occupations is a willingness to GO THE EXTRA MILE; which means the rendering of more and better service than that for which one is paid, and giving it in a *positive mental attitude*.

Search wherever you will for a single sound argument against this principle, and you will not find it; nor will you find a single instance of enduring success that was not attained in part by its application.

The principle is not the creation of man. It is a part of Nature's handiwork, for its is obvious that every living creature below the intelligence of man is forced to apply the principle in order to survive.

Man may disregard the principle if he chooses, but he cannot do so and at the same time enjoy the fruits of enduring success.

Observe how Nature applies this principle in the production of food that grows from the soil, where the farmer is forced to GO THE EXTRA MILE by clearing the land, plowing it, and planting the seed at the right time of the year, for none of which he receives any pay in advance.

But, observe that if does his work in harmony with Nature's laws, and performs the necessary amounts of labor, Nature takes over the job where the farmer's labor ends, germinates the seed he plants, and develops it into a crop of food.

And, observe thoughtfully this significant fact: For every grain of wheat or corn he plants in the soil Nature yields him perhaps a hundred grains, thus enabling him to benefit by the law of increasing returns.

Nature GOES THE EXTRA MILE by producing enough of everything for her needs, together with a surplus for emergencies and waste; for example, the fruit on the trees, the bloom from which the fruit is grown, frogs in the pond and fish in the seas.

The advantages of the habit of GONG THE EXTRA MILE are definite and understandable. Let us examine some of them and be convinced:

The habit brings the individual to the *favorable attention* of those who can and will provide opportunities for self-advancement.

It tends to make one indispensible, in many different human relationships, and it therefore enables him to command more than average compensation for personal services.

It leads to mental growth and to physical skill and perfection in many forms of endeavor, thereby adding to one's earning capacity.

It enables one to profit by the law of contrast since *the majority of people do not practice the habit.*

It leads to the development of a positive, pleasing mental attitude, which is essential for enduring success.

It tends to develop a keen, alert imagination because it is a habit that inspires one continuously to seek new and better ways of rendering service.

It develops the important quality of personal initiative.

It develops self-reliance and courage.

It serves to build the confidence of others in one's integrity.

It aids the mastery of the destructive habit of procrastination.

It develops definiteness of purpose, ensuring one against the common habit of aimlessness.

There is still another, and a greater reason, for following the habit of GOING THE EXTRA MILE. *It gives one the only logical reason for asking for increased compensation.*

The attitude of the man who follows the habit of GOING THE EXTRA MILE is this: *He recognizes the truth that he is receiving pay for schooling himself for a better position and greater pay!*

This is an asset of which no worker can be cheated, no matter how selfish or greedy his immediate employer may be.

CHAPTER SIX

Love, the True Emancipator of Mankind!

Love is man's greatest experience. It brings one into communication with Infinite Intelligence.

When it is blended with the emotions of sex and romance it may lead one to the higher mountain-peaks of individual achievement through *creative vision*.

The emotions of love, sex, and romance are the three sides of the eternal triangle of achievement known as genius. Nature creates geniuses through no other media.

Love is an outward expression of the spiritual nature of man.

Sex is purely biological, but it supplies the springs of action in all creative effort, from the humblest creation that crawls to the most profound of all creations, man.

When love and sex are combined with the spirit of romance the world may well rejoice, for these are the potentials of the great leaders who are the profound thinkers of the world.

The love of which I speak must not be confused with the emotions of sex, for love in its highest and purest expression is a combination of the eternal triangle, *yet it is greater than any one of its three component parts!*

The love to which I refer is the "élan vital"—the life-giving factor—the spring of action—of all creative endeavors that have lifted mankind to its present state of refinement and culture.

It is the one factor that draws a clear line of demarcation between man and all the creatures of the earth below him. It is the one factor that determines for every man the amount of space he shall occupy in the hearts of his fellowmen.

Love is the solid foundation upon which the first of the Twelve Riches may be built, *a positive mental attitude.* Love is the warp and woof of all the remaining eleven riches. It embellishes all riches and gives them the quality of endurance.

The *habit* of GOING THE EXTRA MILE leads to the attainment of that spirit of love, for there can be no greater expression of love than love that is demonstrated through service rendered completely and unselfishly.

CHAPTER SEVEN

The Master Mind

Definition: *An alliance of two or more minds, blended in a spirit of perfect harmony and cooperation for the attainment of a definite purpose.*

Note well the definition of this principle, for it carries a meaning that provides the key to the attainment of a great personal power.

The Master Mind is the basis of all great achievements, the foundation stone of major importance in all human progress, whether individual or collective.

The key to its power may be found in the word "harmony"!

Without that element, collective effort may constitute cooperation, but it will lack the power that harmony provides through coordination of effort.

The tenets of major importance in connection with the Master Mind are:

1. The Master Mind principle is the medium through which one may procure the full benefit of the *experience, training, education, specialized knowledge, and native ability of others*, just as completely as if their minds were one's own.

2. An alliance of two or more minds a spirit of *perfect* harmony for the attainment of a definite purpose, stimulates each individual mind with a high degree of inspiration, and may become that state of mind known as Faith! (A slight idea of this stimulation and its power is experienced in the relationship of close friendship and in the relationship of love.)

3. Every human brain is both a broadcasting and receiving station for the expression of the vibrations of thought, and the effect of the Master Mind principles stimulates action of thought, through what is commonly known as telepathy, operating through the sixth sense.

4. The Master Mind principle, when actively applied, has the effect of connection one with the subconscious section of the mind, and the subconscious sections of the minds of his allies—a fact that may explain many of the seemingly miraculous results obtained through the Master Mind.

5. The more important human relationships in connection with which one may apply the Master

Mind principle are: (a) marriage, (b) religion, and (c) in connection with one's occupation, profession, or calling.

The Master Mind principle made it possible for Thomas Edison to become a great inventor despite his lack of education and his lack of knowledge of the sciences with which he had to work—a circumstance that offers hope to all who erroneously believe themselves seriously handicapped by a lack of formal education.

There are two general types of Master Mind alliances:

1. Alliance, for purely personal reasons, with one's relatives, religious advisors and friends, where no material gain or objective is sought. *The most important of this type of alliance is that of man and wife.*

2. Alliances for business, professional, and economic advancement, consisting of individuals who have a personal motive in connection with the object of the alliance.

Never neglect forming a Master Mind alliance; great power can be attained in no other way.

CHAPTER EIGHT

Applied Faith

Faith is a royal visitor that enters only the mind that has been properly prepared for it; the mind that has been set in order through *self-discipline*.

In the fashion of all royalty, Faith commands the best room, nay, the finest suite, in the mental dwelling place.

It will not be shunted into servant's quarters, and it will not associate with envy, greed, superstition, hatred, revenge, vanity, doubt, worry, or fear.

Get the full significance of this truth and you will be on the way to an understanding of that mysterious power that has baffled scientists through the ages.

When the mind has been cleared of a *negative mental attitude*, the power of Faith moves in and begins to take possession!

Surely no student of this philosophy will be unfortunate enough to miss this important observation.

Let us turn now to analysis of Faith, although we must approach the subject with full recognition that Faith is a power that has defied analysis by the entire scientific world.

Faith is a state of mind that might properly be called the "mainspring of the soul" through which one's aims, desires, and purposes may be translated into their physical or financial equivalent.

Previously we observed that great power may be attained by the application of (1) the habit of GOING THE EXTRA MILE, (2) Definiteness of Purpose, and (3) the Master Mind. But that power is feeble in comparison with that which is available through the combined application of these principles with the state of mind known as Faith.

We have already observed that *capacity for faith* is one of the Twelve Riches. Let us now recognize the means by which this "capacity" may be filled with that strange power that has been the main bulwark of civilization, the chief cause of all human progress, the guiding spirit of all constructive human endeavor.

Let us remember that Faith is a state of mind that may be enjoyed only by those who have learned the art of taking *full and complete control* of their minds! This is the one and only prerogative right over which an individual has been given complete control.

Faith expresses its powers only through the mind that has been prepared for it. But the way of preparation is known, and may be attained by all who desire to find it.

The fundamentals of Faith are:

1. Definiteness of purpose supported by personal initiative or *action*.

2. The habit of GOING THE EXTRA MILE in all human relationships.

3. A Master Mind alliance with one or more people who radiate courage based on Faith, and who are suited spiritually and mentally to one's needs in carrying out a given purpose.

4. A positive mind, free from all negatives, such as fear, envy, greed, hatred, jealousy, and superstition. (A positive mental attitude is the first and the most important of the Twelve Riches.)

5. Recognition of the truth that every adversity carries with it the seed of equivalent benefit; that *temporary defeat is not failure* until it has been accepted as such.

6. The habit of affirming one's Definite Major Purpose in life in a ceremony of meditation at least once daily.

7. Recognition of the existence of Infinite Intelligence, which gives orderliness to the universe; that all individuals are minute expressions of this In-

telligence; and as such the individual mind has no limitations except those that are accepted and set up by the individual in his own mind.

8. A careful inventory (in retrospect) of one's past defeats and adversities, which will reveal the truth that all such experiences carry the seed of an equivalent benefit.

9. Self-respect expressed through harmony with one's own conscience.

These are the fundamentals of major importance that prepare the mind for the expression of Faith. Their application calls for no degree of superiority, but application does call for intelligence and *a keen thirst for truth and justice.*

Remember: faith fraternizes only with the mind that is positive!

How to Demonstrate the Power of Faith

1. Know what you want and determine what you have to give in return for it.

2. When you affirm the objects of your desires, through prayer, inspire your imagination to see

yourself already in possession of them, and act precisely as if you were in the physical possession thereof. (Remember the possession of anything first takes place mentally.)

3. Keep the mind open at all times for *guidance from within,* and when you are inspired by hunches to modify your plans or to move on a new plan, move without hesitancy or doubt.

4. When overtaken by temporary defeat, as you may be overtaken many times, remember that man's Faith is tested in many ways, and your defeat may be only one of your "testing periods." Therefore, accept defeat as an inspiration to greater effort, and carry on with belief that you will succeed.

5. Any negative state of mind will destroy the capacity for Faith and result in a negative climax of any affirmation you may express. Your state of mind is everything; therefore take possession of your mind and clear it completely of all unwanted interlopers that are unfriendly to Faith, and keep it cleared, no matter what may be the cost in effort.

6. Learn to give expression to your power of Faith by writing out a clear description of your Definite Major Purpose in life and using it as the basis of your daily meditation.

7. Associate with your Definite Major Purpose as many as possible of the nine basic motives, described previously.

8. Write out a list of all the benefits and advantages you expect to derive from the attainment of the object of your Definite Major Purpose, and call these into your mind many times daily, thereby making your mind "success conscious." (This is commonly called autosuggestion.)

9. Associate yourself, as far as possible, with people who are in sympathy with your Definite Major Purpose; people who are in harmony with you, and inspire them to encourage you in every way possible.

10. Let not a single day pass without making at least one definite move toward the attainment of your Definite Major Purpose. Remember, "Faith without works is dead."

11. Choose some prosperous person of self-reliance and courage as your "pacemaker," and make up your mind not only to keep up with that person, but to excel him. Do this silently, without mentioning your plan to anyone. (Boastfulness will be fatal to your success, as Faith has nothing in common with vanity or self-love.)

12. Surround yourself with books, pictures, wall mottoes, and other suggestive reminders of self-reliance founded upon Faith as it has been demonstrated by other people, thus building around yourself an atmosphere of prosperity and achievement. This habit will be fruitful of stupendous results.

13. Adopt a policy of never evading or running away from unpleasant circumstances, but recognize such circumstances and build a counter-fire against them right where they overtake you. You will discover that recognition of such circumstances, without fear of their consequence, is nine-tenths of the battle in mastering them.

14. Recognize the truth that everything worth having has a definite price. The price of Faith, among other things, is eternal vigilance in carrying out these simple instructions. Your watchword must be PERSISTENCE!

These are the steps that lead to the development and maintenance of a *positive mental attitude*, the only one in which Faith will abide. They are steps that lead to riches of both mind and spirit as well as riches of the purse. Fill your mind with this kind of mental food.

CHAPTER NINE

The Law of Cosmic Habitforce

We now come to the analysis of the greatest of all of Nature's laws, the law of Cosmic Habitforce!

Briefly described, the law of Cosmic Habitforce is Nature's method of giving fixation to all habits so that they may carry on automatically once they have been set into motion—the habits of men the same as the habits of the universe.

Every man is where he is and what he is because of his established habits of thought and deed. The purpose of this entire philosophy is to aid the individual in the formation of the kind of habits that will transfer him from where he is to where wishes to be.

Every scientist, and many laymen, know that Nature maintains a perfect balance between all the elements of matter and energy throughout the universe; that the entire universe is operated through an inexorable system of orderliness and habits that never vary, and cannot be altered by any form of human endeavor; that the five known realities of the universe are: (1) Time, (2) Space, (3) Energy, (4) Matter, and (5) Intelligence; these shaped the other known realities into orderliness and system based upon *fixed habits.*

These are nature's building-blocks with which she creates a grain of sand or the largest stars that float through space, and every other thing known to man, or that the mind of man can conceive.

These are the known realities, but not everyone has taken the time or the interest to ascertain that Cosmic Habitforce is the particular application of Energy with which Nature maintains the relationship between the atoms of matter, the stars and the planets in their ceaseless motion onward toward some unknown destiny, the seasons of the year, night and day, sickness and health, life and death. Cosmic Habitforce is the medium through which all habits and all human relationships are maintained in varying degrees of permanence, and the medium through which thought is translated into its physical equivalent in response to the desires and purposes of the individual.

But these truths are capable of proof, and one may count that hour sacred during which he discovers the inescapable truth that man is only an instrument through which higher powers than his own are projecting themselves. This entire philosophy is designed to lead one to this important discovery, and to enable him to make use of the knowledge it reveals, *by placing himself in harmony with the unseen forces of the universe, which may carry him inevitably into the success side of the great River of Life.*

The hour of this discovery should bring him within easy reach of the Master Key to all Riches!

Cosmic Habitforce is Nature's Comptroller through which all other natural laws are coordinated, organized, and operated through orderliness and system. Therefore it is the greatest of all natural laws.

The law of Cosmic Habitforce is Nature's own creation. It is the one universal principle through which order and system and harmony are carried out in the entire operation of the universe, from the largest star that hangs in the heavens to the smallest atoms of matter.

It is a power that is equally available to the weak and the strong, the rich and poor, the sick and well. It provides the solution to all human problems.

The major purpose of the seventeen principles of this philosophy is that of aiding the individual to adapt himself to the power of Cosmic Habitforce by self-discipline in connection with the formation of his habits of thought.

Let us turn now to a brief review of these principles, so that we may understand their relationship to Cosmic Habitforce. Let us observe how these principles are so related that they blend together and form the Master Key that unlocks the doors to the solution of all problems.

The analysis begins with the first principle of the philosophy:

1. THE HABIT OF GOING THE EXTRA MILE. This principle is given first because it aids in conditioning the mind for the rendering of useful service. And this condition prepares the way for the second principle—

2. DEFINITENESS OF PURPOSE. With the aid of this principle one may give organized direction to the principle of Going the Extra Mile, and make sure that it leads in the direction of his major purpose and becomes cumulative in its effects. These two principles alone will take anyone far up the ladder of achievement, but those who are aiming for the higher goals of life will need much help on the way, and this help is available through the application of the third principle—

3. THE MASTER MIND. Through the application of this principle one begins to experience a new and greater sense of power which is not available to the

individual mind, as it bridges one's personal deficiencies and provides him, when necessary, with any portion of the combined knowledge of mankind, which has accumulated throughout the ages. But this sense of power will not be complete until one acquires of art of receiving guidance through the fourth principle—

4. APPLIED FAITH. Here an individual begins to tune in to the powers of Infinite Intelligence, which is a benefit that is available only to the person who has conditioned his mind to receive it. Here the individual begins to take full possession of his own mind by mastering all fears, worries, and doubts, by recognizing his oneness with the source of all power. These four principles have been rightly called the "Big Four" because they are capable of providing more power than the average man needs to carry him to great heights of personal achievement. But these are adequate only for the very few who have other needed qualities of success, such as those provided by the fifth principle.

5. PLEASING PERSONALITY. A pleasing personality enables a man to sell himself and his ideas to others. Hence, it is an essential for all who desire to become the guiding influence in a Master Mind alliance. But observe carefully how definitely the

four preceding principles tend to give one a pleasing personality. These five principles are capable of providing one with stupendous personal power, but not enough power to ensure him against defeat, for defeat is a circumstance that every man meets many times throughout his life; hence the necessity of understanding and applying the sixth principle—

6. HABIT OF LEARNING FROM DEFEAT. Notice that this principle begins with the word "habit," which means that it must be accepted and applied as a matter of habit, under all circumstances of defeat. In this principle may be found hope sufficient to inspire a man to make a fresh start when his plans go astray, as go astray they must at one time or another.

7. CREATIVE VISION. This principle enables one to look into the future and to judge it by a comparison with the past, and to build new and better plans for attaining his hopes and aims through the workshop of his imagination. And here, for the first time perhaps, a man may discover his sixth sense and begin to draw upon it for the knowledge which is not available through the organized sources of human experience and accumulated knowledge. But, in order to make sure that he puts this bene-

fit to practical use he must embrace and apply the eighth principle—

8. PERSONAL INITIATIVE. This is the principle that starts action and keeps it moving toward definite ends. It insures one against the destructive habits of procrastination, laziness, and indifference. An approximation of the importance of this principle may be had by recognizing that it is the "habit-producer" in connection with the seven preceding principles, for it is obvious that the application of no principle may become a *habit* expect by the application of personal initiative. The importance of this principle may be further evaluated by recognition of the fact that it is the sole means by which a man may exercise full and complete control over the only thing the Creator has given him to control, *the power of his own thoughts.* But personal initiative is sometimes misdirected. Therefore it needs supplemental guidance from the ninth principle—

9. ACCURATE THINKING. Accurate thinking not only insures against the misdirection of personal initiative, but it also insures against errors of judgment, guesswork, and premature decisions. It also protects one against the influence of his own undependable emotions by modifying them

through the power of reason. The individual who has mastered these nine principles will find himself in possession of tremendous power, but personal power may be, and often is, dangerous if it is not controlled and directed through application of the tenth principle—

10. SELF-DISCIPLINE. Self-discipline cannot be had for the mere asking. Nor can it be acquired quickly. It is the product of carefully established and carefully maintained habits, which in many instances can be acquired only by many years of painstaking effort. So we have come to the point at which the power of the will must be brought into action, *for self-discipline is solely a product of the will.* Numberless men have risen to great power by the application of the nine preceding principles only to meet with ultimate failure. Self-discipline must begin with the application of the eleventh principle—

11. CONCENTRATION OF ENDEAVOR. The power of concentration is also a product of the will. It is so closely related to self-discipline that the two have been called the twin brothers of this philosophy. Concentration saves one from the dissipation of his energies, and aids him in keeping his mind focused upon the object of his Definite Major Purpose until it has been taken over by the

subconscious section of the mind and there made ready for translation into its physical equivalent, through the law of Cosmic Habitforce. It is the camera's eye of the imagination through which the detailed outline of one's aims and purposes are recorded in the subconscious; hence it is indispensable. But even these powers are not sufficient for every circumstance; there are times when one must have the friendly cooperation of many people, such as customers, clients, or voters, all of which may be had through the application of the twelfth principle—

12. COOPERATION. Cooperation differs from the Master Mind principle in that it is a human relationship that is needed, and may be had, without a definite alliance with others based upon a complete fusion of the minds. Without cooperation of others one cannot attain success in the higher brackets of personal achievement, for cooperation is the means of major value by which one may extend the space he occupies in the minds of others, which is sometimes called goodwill. Cooperation is attained more freely and willingly by the application of the thirteenth principle—

13. ENTHUSIASM. Enthusiasm is a contagious state of mind that not only aids one in gaining the coop-

eration of others, but more importantly, it inspires the individual to draw upon and use the power of his own imagination. It inspires action also in the expression of personal initiative, and it leads to the habit of concentration of endeavor. Moreover, it is one of the qualities of major importance in a pleasing personality, and it makes easy the application of the principle of Going the Extra Mile. In addition to all these benefits, enthusiasm gives force and conviction to the spoken word. Enthusiasm is the product of *motive*, but it is difficult to maintain without the aid of the fourteenth principle—

14. THE HABIT OF HEALTH. Sound physical health provides a suitable housing place for the operation of the mind; hence it is an essential for enduring success, assuming that the word "success" shall embrace all of the requirements for happiness. Here again the word "habit" comes into prominence, for sound health begins with a "health consciousness" that can be developed only by the right habits of living. Sound health provides the basis for enthusiasm, and enthusiasm encourages sound health; so the two are like the hen and the egg: no one can determine which came into existence first, but everyone knows that both are essential for

the production of either. Health and enthusiasm are like that. Both are essential for human progress and happiness.

15. BUDGETING TIME AND MONEY. Nearly everyone wishes to spend time and money freely, but budget and conserve them—never! However, independence and freedom of body and mind, the two great desires of all mankind, cannot become enduring realities without the self-discipline of a strict budgeting system. Hence, this principle is an essential part of the philosophy of individual achievement.

16. THE GOLDEN RULE *APPLIED*. Note the emphasis on the word "applied." Belief in the soundness of the Golden Rule is not enough. To be of enduring benefit, and in order that it may serve as a safe guide in the use of personal power, it must be applied as a matter of habit, in all human relationships. Quite an order, this! But the benefits that are available through the application of this profound rule of human relations are worthy of the efforts necessary to develop it into a habit. The penalties for failure to live by this rule are too numerous to describe. Now we have attained the ultimate in personal power, and we have provided ourselves

with the necessary insurance against its misuse. What we need from here on out is the means by which this power may be made permanent during our entire lifetime. We shall climax this philosophy, therefore, with the only known principle by which we may attain this desired end—the seventeenth and last principle of this philosophy—

17. COSMIC HABITFORCE. *Cosmic Habitforce* is the principle by which all habits are fixed and made permanent in varying degrees. As stated, it is the comptrolling principle of the entire philosophy, into which the preceding sixteen principles blend and become a part. And it is the comptrolling principle of all natural laws of the universe. It is the principle that gives the *fixation of habit* in the application of the principles of this philosophy. Mere understanding of the sixteen preceding principles will not lead anyone to the attainment of personal power. The principles must be understood and applied as a matter of strict habit, and habit is the sole work of the law of Cosmic Habitforce. Cosmic Habitforce is synonymous with the great River of Life, for it consists of a negative and a positive potentiality, as do all forms of energy.

You now have at your command a *complete philosophy* of life that is sufficient for the solution of every individual problem. It is a philosophy of principles, some combination of which has been responsible for every individual success in every occupation or calling.

Self-Discipline

S elf-discipline is one of the Twelve Riches, but it is much more; it is an important prerequisite for the attainment of all riches, including freedom of mind and body, power and fame, and all the material things that are called wealth.

It is the sole means by which one may focus the mind upon the objective of a Definite Major Purpose until the law of Cosmic Habitforce takes over the pattern of that purpose and begins to translate it into its material equivalent.

It is the key to the volitional *power of the will* and the *emotions of the heart*, for it is the means by which these two may be mastered and balanced, one against the other, and directed to definite ends in *accurate thinking*.

It is the directing force in the maintenance of a Definite Major Purpose.

Also it operates entirely through the functioning system of the mind. Therefore, let us examine this system so that we may understand the factors of which it consists.

The Ten Factors of the "Mechanism" of Thought

The mind operates through ten factors, some of which operate automatically, while others must be directed through voluntary effort. *Self-disciple is the sole means of this direction.*

The ten factors are:

1. INFINITE INTELLIGENCE. The source of all power of thought, which operates automatically, but it may be organized and directed to definite ends through DEFINITENESS OF PURPOSE. Infinite intelligence may be likened to a great reservoir of water that overflows continuously, its branches flowing in small streams in many directions, and giving life to all vegetation and all living things. That portion of the stream that gives life to man supplies him also with the power of thought.

2. THE CONSCIOUS MIND. The individual mind functions through two departments. One is known as the conscious section of the mind; the other the

subconscious. It is the opinion of psychologists that these two sections are comparable to an iceberg, the visible portion above the waterline representing the conscious section, and the invisible portion below the waterline representing the subconscious. Therefore it is obvious that the conscious section of the mind—that portion with which we consciously and voluntarily turn on the power of thought—is but a small portion of the whole, consisting of perhaps one-fifth of the available mind power. All the other essential functions are performed by the subconscious mind, which also serves as the connecting link between the conscious mind and *Infinite Intelligence.* It may be likened to the spigot of the consciousness mind, through which (by its control through self-discipline) more thought power may be turned on. Or it may be likened to a rich garden spot wherein may be planted and germinated the seed of any desired idea.

3. THE FACULTY OF WILLPOWER. The power of the will is the "boss" of all departments of the mind. It has the power to modify, change, or balance all thinking habits, and its decisions are final and irrevocable except by itself. It is the power that puts the emotions of the heart under control, and it is subject to direction only by self-discipline. In

this connection, it may be likened to the Chairman of the Board of Directors whose decisions are final. It takes its orders from the conscious mind, *but recognizes no other authority*.

4. THE FACULTY OF REASON. This is the "presiding judge" of the conscious section of the mind, which may pass judgment on all its ideas, plans, and desires, and it will do so if it is directed by self-discipline. But its decisions can be set aside by the power of the will, or modified by the power of the emotions when the will does not interfere. Let us here take note that all accurate thinking requires the cooperation of the faculty of reason, *although it is a requirement which not more than one person in every ten thousand respects*. This is why there are so few accurate thinkers. Most so-called thinking is the work of the emotions without the guiding influence of self-discipline; without relationship to either the power of the will or the faculty of reason.

5. THE FACULTY OF THE EMOTIONS. This is the source of most of the actions of the mind, the seat of most of the thoughts released by the conscious section of the mind. The emotions are tricky and undependable and may be very dangerous if they are not modified by the faculty of reason under the direction of the faculty of the will.

However, the faculty of the emotions is not to be condemned because of its unpredictability, for it is the source of all enthusiasm, imagination, and Creative Vision, and it may be directed by self-discipline to the development of these essentials of individual achievement. The direction may be given by modification of the emotions through the faculties of the will and the reason. *Accurate thinking* is not possible without complete mastery of the emotions. The emotions that are most important and most dangerous are: (1) the emotion of sex, (2) the emotion of love, and (3) the emotion of fear. *These are the emotions that produce the major portion of all human activities.* The emotions of love and sex are creative. When controlled and directed they inspire one with imagination and creative vision of stupendous proportions. If they are not controlled and directed they may lead one to indulge in tremendous follies.

6. THE FACULTY OF IMAGINATION. This is the workshop wherein are shaped and fashioned all desires, ideas, plans, and purposes, together with the means of attaining them. Through organized use and self-discipline the imagination may be developed to the status of Creative Vision. But the faculty of the imagination, like the faculty of the

emotions, is tricky and undependable if it is not controlled and directed by self-discipline. Without control it often dissipates the power of thought in useless, impractical, and destructive activities. *Uncontrolled imagination is the stuff that daydreams are made of!*

7. THE FACULTY OF CONSCIENCE. The conscience is the moral guide of the mind, and its major purpose is modifying the individual's aims and purposes so that they harmonize with the moral laws of nature and of mankind. The conscience is the twin-brother of the faculty of reason in that it gives discrimination and guidance to the reason when reason is in doubt. The conscience functions as a cooperative guide only so long as it is respected and followed. If it is neglected, or its mandates are rejected, it finally becomes a conspirator instead of a guide, and often volunteers to justify man's destructive habits. Thus the dual nature of the conscience makes it necessary for one to direct it through strict self-discipline.

8. THE SIXTH SENSE. This is the "broadcasting station" of the mind through which one automatically sends and receives the vibrations of thought commonly known as telepathy. It is the medium through which all thought impulses and hunches

are received. And it is closely related to, or perhaps it may be a part of, the subconscious. The sixth sense is the medium through which Creative Vision operates. It is the medium through which all basically new ideas are revealed. And it is the major asset of the minds of all who are known as geniuses.

9. THE MEMORY. This is the filing cabinet of the brain, wherein is stored all thought impulses, all experiences, and all sensations that reach the brain through the five physical senses.. And it may be the filing cabinet of all impulses of thought that reach the mind through the sixth sense. The memory is tricky and undependable unless it is organized and directed by self-discipline.

10. THE FIVE PHYSICAL SENSES. These are the physical arms of the brain through which it contacts the external world and acquires information. The physical senses are not reliable, and therefore require constant self-discipline. Under any kind of intense emotional activity the senses become confused and unreliable. The five senses are easily deceived. And they are deceived daily by the common experiences of life. Under the emotion of fear the physical senses often create monstrous "ghosts" that have no existence except in the faculty of the

imagination, and there is no fact of life that they will not exaggerate or distort when fear prevails. In this sense, fear is the archenemy of mankind.

Before leaving the analysis of self-discipline, which deals entirely with the mechanism of thought, let us briefly describe some of the known facts and habits of thought in order that we may acquire the art of accurate thinking.

1. All thought (whether it is positive or negative, good or bad, accurate or inaccurate) tends to clothe itself in its physical equivalent, and it does so by inspiring one with ideas, plans, and the means of attaining desired ends, through logical and natural methods.

2. Through the application of self-discipline thought can be influenced, controlled, and directed through transmutation to a desired end, by the development of voluntary habits suitable for the attainment of any given end.

3. The power of thought (through the aid of the subconscious) has control over every cell of the body and all the effects therein. These functions are carried on automatically but many may be stimulated by voluntary aid.

4. All of man's achievements begin in the form of thought, organized into plans, aims, and purposes, and expressed in terms of physical action. All action is inspired by one or more of the nine basic motives.

5. The entire power of the mind operates through the conscious and subconscious. The conscious section is under the control of the individual; the subconscious is controlled by Infinite Intelligence and is the medium of communication between Infinite Intelligence and the conscious mind.

6. Both the conscious and subconscious function in response to fixed habits, whether the habits are voluntary or involuntary.

7. The majority of one's thoughts are inaccurate because they are inspired by personal opinions that are reached without examination of the facts, or because of bias, prejudice, fear, and emotional excitement.

8. The first step in accurate thinking is that of separating facts from hearsay evidence and emotional reactions. The second step is that of separating facts, after they have been identified as such, into two classes: important and unimportant. An important fact can be used to help you attain your major purpose. All other facts are relatively unimportant.

9. Desire, based on a definite motive, is the beginning of all voluntary thought action associated with individual achievement. The presence in the mind of any intense desire tends to stimulate the faculty of the imagination with the purpose of creating ways and means of attaining the desire.

These are some of the more important of the known facts concerning the greatest of mysteries, the mystery of human thought, and they indicate clearly that accurate thinking is attainable only by the strictest habits of self-discipline.

The lights were now dimmed. The masked rich man from Happy Valley finished speaking and disappeared into the darkness as mysteriously as he had arrived, but he had given every member of that huge audience a new birth of hope, faith, and courage.

Remember it is profoundly significant that the only thing over which you have complete control is your own mental attitude!

If the rich man from Happy Valley has brought you nothing but this great truth he has provided you with a source to riches of incomparable value; for this is the Master Key to Riches!

NAPOLEON HILL was born in 1883 in Wise County, Virginia. He was employed as a secretary, a reporter for a local newspaper, the manager of a coalmine and a lumberyard, and attended law school, before he began working as a journalist for *Bob Taylor's Magazine,* an inspirational and general-interest journal. In 1908, the job led to his interviewing steel magnate Andrew Carnegie. The encounter, Hill said, changed the course of his life. Carnegie believed success could be distilled into principles that anyone could follow, and urged Hill to interview the greatest industrialists, financiers, and inventors of the era to discover these principles. Hill accepted the challenge, which lasted more than twenty years and formed the building block for *Think and Grow Rich.* Hill dedicated the rest of his life to documenting and refining the principles of success. After a long career as an author, magazine publisher, lecturer, and consultant to business leaders, the motivational pioneer died in 1970 in South Carolina.

MITCH HOROWITZ, who abridged and introduced this volume, is the PEN Award-winning author of books including *Occult America* and *The Miracle Club: How Thoughts Become Reality. The Washington Post* says Mitch "treats esoteric ideas and movements with an even-handed intellectual studiousness that is too often lost in today's raised-voice discussions." Follow him @MitchHorowitz.